Holiness Horizons

A

PURVIEW

OF

SANCTIFICATION

NELSON S. PERDUE

First Printing March 2007

Second Printing October 2009

Whispering Pines Publishing
11013 Country Pines Road
Shoals, IN 47581

ISBN: 978-1-934447-04-8

TABLE OF CONTENTS

PREFACE

When I go to a restaurant I like to look over the menu before ordering. What is listed that looks particularly appetizing? When I pick up a book I usually look at the table of contents to see if it appears worth reading. When I saw the menu of this book, when I considered what Brother Nelson Perdue has prepared for us, I knew I would appreciate the meal! Now that I have enjoyed it myself, I gladly recommend it to other lovers of God's will for humanity.

This book is a summary of true Biblical holiness. It properly begins with the essential nature of God. The author notes that our Lord created humanity to be like Himself in holiness. Anything contrary to holiness opposes the creative purpose of our loving God. But the offering of Jesus at Calvary makes His creative purpose possible today.

The human race has fallen far short of what God intends it to be. This book tells the way back, describing each step in careful, scriptural detail. The seeker after God's best will find personal guidance here. The honest reader will see answers to false teachings that claim Biblical authority but deny the very purpose of God. The earnest witness to full salvation will learn better how to lead others into the grace provided at Calvary.

Our brother Nelson Perdue is an experienced and faithful evangelist. It has been my privilege to hear him many times in revivals and camp meetings, and to have personal fellowship with him. God is using his preaching, witnessing, and exhortations to lead many into true Scriptural holiness. This book is a thoughtful and thorough presentation of the sanctifying power of our Lord and Savior, Jesus Christ. I am thankful God led our brother to write it.

Dr. Wilfred Fisher

INTRODUCTION

There has been much misinformation on the subject of Entire Sanctification across the years. This has created much opposition and many have objections to the validity of this doctrine. Many learned men and women have written volumes of scholarly works defining this subject, and so the question poses itself, why another book on this subject?

Perhaps the question can be best answered by my own personal testimony. It was fifty years ago, through life's providences and the prevenient grace of God, that I was stricken with the knowledge of my own alienation from God and was without hope in this world. I cried out to God, confessed my sinful state and in faith believing, God for Christ's sake, forgave me of my sins, and immediately I was made aware of His transforming grace. As the song writer put it, *"like sparks from smitten steel,"* I knew God had answered my prayer and lifted the guilt off my soul.

The days that followed were blessed by His presence. However, four weeks later in a study hall in high school, God revealed to me something in my heart that was further back and deeper down then I had ever known. It wasn't an evil act that I had committed but a disposition that was anything but Christ-like. I began to seek God in prayer, and finally, while praying at an altar on a Wednesday night prayer meeting, I found the answer to my prayers when the refining fire of the Holy Ghost cleansed my heart from inbred sin and sanctified me wholly. It was as Wesley's hymn stated, *"My chains fell off; my heart was free. I rose, went forth, and followed thee."* It was then and there that God cleansed my heart and became the Lord of my life. It has now been nearly fifty years since God *regenerated* and *sanctified me wholly,* and I would not exchange one of those days for all of the previous years of my life.

As an evangelist for over 33 years I have been proclaiming this message from the pulpit across the land. It has been my observation that many good Christians have never entered into this experience, and while they have the Holy Spirit, they have never been filled with the Spirit, and have never experienced the freedom that comes through this wonderful work of the Holy Spirit. Their prayer life is powerless, and their spiritual perspective has been clouded, and their service to God has, in a measure, become non-productive. My concern is that if one continues long in this sub-normal Christian walk he will soon believe that it is quite normal to live a spiritually powerless and non-productive life.

It is for this reason that I write this book. It is not a theological treatise born out of great scholarship, but it is simply one beggar telling another beggar where to get food. As the Apostle Paul was commissioned to be both a minister and a witness, so I am writing not only as a minister to a doctrine which I firmly believe but also to an experience that I have received as well as a life that I truly enjoy.

It was following Saul's conversion on the road to Damascus that Ananias was later sent into the city of Damascus where he laid hands on Saul and he received his sight and was filled with the Holy Ghost. This transforming experience turned the persecutor Saul into a witness whose name was changed to Paul. The former murderer of Christians would ultimately be martyred for Christ. His commission was to go to the Gentiles; *"To open their eyes, and to turn them from darkness to light, and from the power of satan unto God, that they may receive <u>forgiveness of sins</u> and <u>inheritance among them which are sanctified by faith that is in me</u>"* (Acts 26:18). Here we see that Paul was commissioned to preach forgiveness for the sinner and also sanctification for the believer. He had experienced both works of grace and was not only a preacher/teacher of them but also a witness to them. Paul was not merely postulating, but he was witnessing. To postulate is to assume something without proof, but to witness is to declare by personal experience.

The central theme of this book will be to present the work of entire sanctification, not only as a duty but also as a present privilege of all Christians. We are convinced that if any honest heart will open God's word and earnestly and obediently seek God's help, he will learn for himself that, "*If any man will do His will, he shall know of the doctrine, whether it be of God, or whether I speak of myself*" (John 7:17).

I.

THE NATURE OF GOD

The greatest fact that we know about God is that He is holy. In the fact of His holiness we have the source of all moral values. The holiness of God is the basis of all righteousness in all moral beings.

God's holiness is original, absolute and eternal. We cannot conceive of the Biblical God in any other character than holy. Our finite minds are unable to comprehend the infinite. As A. W. Tozer reminds us, "One cannot begin to grasp the true meaning of divine holiness by thinking of someone or something very pure and then raising the concept to the highest degree we are capable of. God's holiness is not simply the best we know infinitely bettered. We know nothing like the divine holiness. It stands apart, unique, unapproachable, incomprehensible and unattainable. The natural man is blind to it. He may fear God's power and admire His wisdom, but His holiness he cannot even imagine. Only the Spirit of the Holy One can impart to the human spirit the knowledge of the holy."[1] To speak of God as holy is to affirm His unflawed character. He is without evil, impurity or injustice.

Holiness is the crown and compass of all of God's attributes. Methodist theologian, Thomas N. Ralston said, "Holiness is the substratum of all of His perfections, and the perfections of God are God. They cannot be taken from him, nor can they pertain to any created entity in the vast universe."[2] It is His holiness that prevents His love from becoming indulgence and His justice from becoming tyrannical. Holiness governs all divine attributes, such as mercy, patience, justice, etc. Whether it be the seraphim in Isaiah 6, or the living creatures described in Revelation 4:8, they are not crying "love, love, love," or "power, power, power." They exclaim, *"Holy, holy, holy* is the Lord Almighty." Their threefold cry acknowledges the holiness of the triune God as foundational to His being.

In Leviticus 11:45 we read, *"Ye shall therefore be holy, for I am holy."* Leviticus 19:2 declares, *"I the Lord your God am holy."* In I Peter 1:15, 16 the writer exhorts, *"As He which has called you is holy, so be ye holy in all manner of conversation; because it is written, be ye holy for I am holy."* In His person, power and position God is "the Holy One of Israel," a phrase that Isaiah uses over thirty times in his prophetic book. "Holiness is the essential moral nature of God. This is perfect morality, spotlessness of character, divine purity, absolute freedom from sin of all forms, absolute holiness, Habakuk 1:13."[3]

Following the victory that ended the long struggle between the God of the Israelites and the gods of the Egyptians, the Israelites had a celebration. They sang the Song of Deliverance on freedom's side of the Red Sea. They saw that their God was superior to all other gods in majesty and power, and they beheld His glory. *"Who is like unto thee, O Lord, among the gods? Who is like Thee, glorious in holiness, fearful in praises, doing wonders?"* (Exodus 15:11).

Samuel Chadwick wrote, "Holiness is His glory. It is the essence of the divine quality, and of His attributes it is essential to all the rest. Every essential attribute in a moral being has its active and passive side. Truth-speaking presupposes a truthful person. Behind all the acts and ways of God there is the nature of God. Quality of being is behind the quality of doing. A holy man is behind a holy life, and a

Holy God is the foundation of the will and ways of God. The quality of nature is before the character of conduct, and the character of nature comes before the attribute of power. The holiness of God guarantees the rightness of His thoughts and the integrity of His ways. Therefore those who know His name put their trust in Him. *'Who shall not fear thee, O Lord, and glorify thy name? For thou only art holy'* (Revelation 15:4)."[4]

That God is holy assures us that He always wills for himself and for all men that which is morally right. He is Light and in Him is no darkness; He is Love and He will not endure any carnal hatred; He is Sovereign and will not tolerate rebellion. God's will is a revelation of His character and His character is the standard for His people, "*As He which has called you is holy, so be ye holy*" (I Peter 1:15). By this standard we will all be judged one day.

1. **A. W. Tozer**, *The Knowledge of the Holy*, p. 104

2. **Thomas N. Ralston**, *Elements of Divinity*, p. 31

3. **E. P. Ellyson**, *Doctrinal Studies*, p. 31

4. **Samuel Chadwick**, *Lecture Published in Heart and Life*, November 1949

II.

PRIMITIVE HOLINESS

God created the heavens and the earth and every living creature on the earth. He created the fowls that fly above the earth and the whales and fishes that fill the seas. Then He said, *"Let the earth bring forth...after its kind."* The record of each day's creation ends with the statement, "God saw that it was good" (Genesis 1:1-25). He then proceeded to make man, the acme of His creation. Before creating man God said, *"Let us make man in our image, after our likeness: and let him have dominion over the fish of the sea, and over the fowl of the air, and over the cattle and over all the earth, and over every creeping thing that creepeth upon the earth"* (Genesis 1:26). Here we understand that God made His own holiness the prototype of our own original state.

It was then that *"the Lord formed man of the dust of the ground, and breathed into his nostrils the breath of life; and man became a living soul"* (Genesis 2:7). Adam was given jurisdiction over the Garden of Eden to dress it and keep it. According to Psalm 8:5, God *"crowned him with glory* [dignity] *and honor* [authority]."

What a paradise God gave to Adam and Eve! In the beginning, before the fall, the sun labored for them; the moon lighted up their nights; the flowers brightened and perfumed their pathway; the fruit pleased their taste; the birds sang and inspired them, and the beasts labored for them. In the cool of the day the human pair walked with God and enjoyed sweet fellowship one with another. They were at home with God and at peace with themselves and their environment.

They were benefactors of the peace and glory of God, and there was no such thing as discord; all was harmonious. The peace and glory of God was everywhere to behold. Before their disobedience to God they were unashamed of their nakedness, perhaps because they were robed with His glory.

Adam's holiness consisted of a native disposition in perfect harmony with his moral duty, as a result of his created state. He was, by creation, morally excellent, innocent of any wrong in being or doing. He had to confirm that created state by a decision and action to obey God when tempted to rebel.

In the Garden of Eden man was placed on probation. God gave him vast permissions and privileges, but He placed before him a prohibition: *"And the Lord God commanded the man saying, of every tree of the garden thou mayest freely eat: But of the tree of the knowledge of good and evil, thou shalt not eat of it: for in the day that thou eatest thereof thou shalt surely die"* (Genesis 2:16, 17).

It is this freedom of choice that makes man a moral creature. Otherwise he could never be held accountable for his actions either good or bad. He was given the power of choice, but the power to do a thing does not make doing it necessary or right. The serpent tried to appeal to Eve's reason when he asked, *"Yea, hath God said, ye shall not eat of every tree of the garden?"* It was not only the first question recorded in the Bible, but it was a question intended to cast aspersion on the integrity of God and His word. However, God's command did not put reason on trial. Man's obedience to God's word was the target of trial. In response to this command Adam would determine whether he was going to choose God's will and believe God's word or seek independence of

God by rejecting His word and asserting his own will. Oswald Chambers said that the essence of sin is simply "my right to my will to myself." Sin shines forth in man's self-will, self-love, self-shielding, self-aggrandizement and self-centeredness. The consequence of Adam's disobedience has had its ramifications in the human tragedy and man's dilemma even to this very day.

One man described the ramifications of sin thus: "Sin is an immense river running through the secret channels of hell. It broke out in the Garden of Eden. Ever enlarging, this river flows on around the world; no flowers grow on its banks; no foliage waves beside its murky tide; everlasting lightnings pencil every wave, and hell's terrific thunder bounds from bank to bank with awful crash. Surely no one would visit this awful place; but alas, its shores are lined from source to mouth with human wretches. They crowd to plunge into this fearful tide: all sexes, all colors, and all classes. The mother decks her daughter in the height of fashion, and side by side they plunge into the stream. Into this stream the young man thoughtlessly and laughingly runs. The old man follows, with hoary locks streaming in the wind like the shredded rigging of a storm-ridden ship; he pauses a moment on the verge, but is soon hurled into the seething tide."[1]

What a devastating picture he paints of the plague on the human race called sin. Sin is not a legitimate part of us; it is an abnormal condition, a poisonous malady, a parasite of the soul and a moral deformity planted in us because of Adam's disobedience. Men and women shun smallpox, diphtheria and any other diseases that prey on the physical body, yet they recklessly throw themselves into the slimy embrace of sin. This certainly speaks of the mystery of iniquity.

Why would God bestow upon man this awful capacity to sin? Evidently God did not want to be served by robots. He wanted a creature whom He could love, and one who would reflect His image and reciprocate that love. If love could be coerced it would lose it meaning and value. Freedom of choice gives virtue and meaning to a relationship of love.

The holy God created a human being who possessed freedom to make choices, and this fact made possible the wrong use of such power, which in turn gave birth to evil. Thus the creation of moral beings capable of righteousness made possible the evil for which man is responsible. Capacity in itself is amoral, but the use a free being makes of capacity lends moral quality to decisions and actions.

God did not create the devil or the sinner. God created angels and humans as holy beings and gave them power to remain holy. However, a holy angel by his rebellion against God became a devil, and a holy man rebelled against the will of His Creator, broke the filial relation of sonship, gave birth to sin in the human family and thus became filial in his relation to the devil.

When Adam sinned he forfeited his holy estate and habitat and disinherited the entire human race. When Adam could not master himself and his own will, he lost mastery over all creation. As a result of his disobedience his crown rolled in the dust, and his honor was tarnished and stained. Fear now entered into the picture, and for the first time Adam and Eve recognized their nakedness and tried to hide from God. Creation that once submitted willingly to man's dominion now must be subdued by force because man has forfeited his dignity and dominion. God pronounced judgment on the serpent, and He revealed to Adam the consequence of his disobedience, not only for his immediate family but for the whole human race. Sin and death have now been passed on to all of Adam's posterity. Adam and

Eve were immediately expelled from the paradise of Eden, and God placed a flaming sword at the gate to keep them from re-entering the garden and partaking of the tree of life.

Sin is here because free beings, created to use their freedom in accord with the perfect will of their Creator, used that power to rebel against the word and will of God and took their own way instead of His way. This act brought about an estrangement from God, and man became alienated from his Creator. As a result of his deprivation he progressively became more and more depraved in his nature. Sin is now everybody's problem; yea everybody's only problem because every other dilemma that man wrestles with springs from the sin problem in the heart. All are now born with what A. W. Tozer called the seed of their own disintegration. It is verified in David's penitential prayer in Psalms 51:5, where he confesses, *"Behold I was shapen in iniquity; and in sin did my mother conceive me."*

1. **William Elbert Munsey**, *Sermons and Lectures,* Sermon Entitled, "Retribution" pp. 253-254

III.

SIN: ANTITHESIS OF HOLINESS

God foresaw the possibility of man's fall into sin and made provision for his rescue, a provision consummated in the death of Christ on the cross. In creation God had only to breathe to give man life but in redemption God had to *bleed* in order to provide for him eternal life. Revelation 13:18 speaks of Jesus as *"the Lamb slain from the foundation of the world."* In other words, God placed a floor under Adam's feet, giving him and his posterity time to return to God so that He might redeem and restore man to his holy image. As Joseph H. Smith wrote, "The slaying of the Lamb from God's eternal thought and provision, from the foundation of the world, has unconditionally secured man a parole and has deferred execution of sentence. This short tenure of life on earth is time to give opportunity for man to seek the shelter of Calvary's cross."[1] We are admonished by Amos in chapter 4:12 to *"prepare to meet thy God, O Israel."*

Following the fall of man in the Garden, God immediately set the plan of salvation into motion. This plan unfolded through the ages and finally was fulfilled when Jesus, the Lamb of God, cried out, *"It is finished,"* and died upon the cross. It was there that He made full provision to save mankind from both the fruit and the root of sin. He now sits at the right hand of the Father, acting as our Mediator and our Advocate before the Father. My purpose in this book is to uncover man's sin problem and re-discover God's salvation plan.

21

In considering man's sin problem, I quote from Richard S. Taylor. "The doctrines relating to sin form the center around which we build our entire theological system... As Christians, if our conception of sin is faulty, our whole superstructure will be one error built on another, each one more absurd than the last, yet each one necessary if it is to fit in consistently with the whole erroneous scheme. If we are to end right we must begin right, and to begin right we must grapple with the question of sin in its doctrinal significance until we have grasped the scriptural facts relating to sin in all of its phases."[2] Practically all heresy and confusion concerning the doctrine of holiness grow out of a misconception of sin. The basis of all that we know about sin, and the source of our understanding of sin, comes from the Bible which is the ultimate authority on the subject.

I am not writing a theological discourse on sin, but I seek to discuss the sin problem with simplicity and clarity in this chapter. There are some who teach that any deviation from an absolute standard of perfect behavior is sin. This would include all mistakes and failures that arise from infirmities of mind and body. However, rightly understood, infirmities are grounded in the body but sin is grounded in the carnal nature. The body can be disciplined and brought under God's mastery but the carnal nature *"is not subject to the law of God, neither indeed can be"* (Romans 8:7). The Apostle Paul said, *"Most gladly therefore will I rather glory in my infirmities, that the power of Christ may rest upon me"* (2 Corinthians 12:9). Therefore we must distinguish the difference between sin and infirmities. I'm confident that Paul never gloried in his sin. Sin is twofold in its nature, it is a *deliberate act*. John, in his first epistle states that *"sin is the transgression of the law"* or sin is lawlessness *(anomia)*. It is a willful violation of the known law of God. Sin is also a *diseased state* which speaks of a heart condition, a corrupt nature which prompts outward acts of sin. Sin in one's conduct is the result of one's sinful character.

Therefore the act of transgression needs to be confessed, repented of and forsaken in order to receive God's forgiveness; there is also a disposition in the heart that prompts one to transgress God's law, this disposition needs to be cleansed by the atoning blood of Christ. A truism affirms that a tree is not an apple tree because it bears apples, but it bears apples because it is an apple tree. So man is not a sinner because he commits sin, but rather, he commits sin because he is a sinner. The root always precedes the fruit.

It is this innate principle of sin in man that prompts every evil act that he commits. It is called the carnal mind, and it always *"minds the things of the flesh"* (Romans 8:5-8). It is lawless in its nature and this incorrigible principle will defy all authority except the dictates of its own will and desire. It is the fertile seed-bed of all evil and holds high treason against the government of God, for it is an aversion to His holiness and truth and to all that is upright and good.

Jesus acknowledged this principle in man when He delivered His great Sermon on the Mount. He taught that lust was adultery if it never got beyond the look or the desire. He said that hate-filled anger was murder if there never was a drop of blood shed. He taught that sin goes far beyond the act of evil, but it involves the motives and intents of the heart. Sin is portrayed as a ruler in the heart that holds the mind and the members of the body under absolute control. It depicts man as a slave to the passions, appetites and affections of the world. When one recognizes the twofold nature of sin, he will realize the need of two works of grace. We will endeavor to show that God, through the atoning work of Calvary, has provided a double cure for man's sin problem.

It should further be noted that when God's word speaks of minding the things of the flesh, it is not talking about the physical body, nor is it saying that the physical body is the seat of sin. This is what the Gnostics taught, and the teaching is very prominent today. Many believe and teach that sin resides in the body and that all matter is evil, and therefore man can never be fully delivered from sin as long as he is in the body. This teaching makes death the deliverer from sin rather than the efficacious blood of Christ. It makes God the originator of sin in creation, and one would have to believe that Jesus was sinful while in the flesh in this world if he subscribed to such teaching. The word "flesh" in Romans 8:8, is not speaking of the physical body but rather the *"carnal mind."* In the very next verse, the Apostle Paul, speaking to those in the physical body says, *"Ye are not in the flesh, but in the Spirit."*

As we move through the succeeding pages of this book I hope to present to you that carnality is not the standard of Christianity; holiness is the standard. It is not an expression of self-will but commitment to God's will. A wrong concept of sin is the result of a wrong concept of our holy God. It is only in the light of His holiness that we are able to identify man's sin problem. When the doctrine of holiness is held in disrepute, it is an affront against the divine character of God. It belittles the work of the atonement and diminishes the efficacy of the blood. It also undermines the justice of God, and Christian ethics and morality go awry.

1. **Joseph H. Smith**, *The Pentecostal Herald*, February 6, 1957

2. **Richard S. Taylor**, *The Right Conception of Sin*, pp. 9, 10

IV.

HOLINESS: GOD'S SUPREME OBJECTIVE IN REDEMPTION

God's objective in redemption is no different than His objective in creation. His plan in creation was to make man in His image and after His likeness. In redemption He plans to redeem man and restore him to that lost image. We will endeavor to present the various components of the redemptive scheme. The call to holiness is a basic truth of God's plan and the provision of Calvary. All truth in any realm of thought is exclusive of error. It is true that God's call to holiness is based upon the <u>character of God</u>. *"Be ye holy; for I am holy."* This is also confirmed by the <u>charter of God</u>. *"It is written, be ye holy."* It is written in the law, prophecies, psalms, prayers, and promises of His Word. What is required and recorded, like all other truths in the realm of divine grace, is proven by personal Christian experience. Therefore the doctrines of divine grace are for the cure of man's sin problem—his disobedience, disposition, as well as his depravity. The experiences of forgiveness and cleansing of the heart carries with them the knowledge of their truths. No one in possession of the truth and experience of Christian holiness, ever questions the integrity and authority of the Bible as the inspired word of God. The Bible is the source and foundation of our beliefs, and we are admonished to *"earnestly contend for the faith which was once delivered unto the saints"* (Jude 3).

Holiness was the essential quality of man in his creative state and is also God's required and essential quality for man in redemption. This, God provided, through the atoning work of His Son, Christ Jesus, when He died on the cross. Our Holy God is eternal and immutable and as a result of these two attributes there has never been any variation in His character or deviation in His purpose. His desire for man's destiny is that he be in heaven, for it is promised in John 3:16 that *"whosoever believeth in Him shall not perish but have everlasting life."* His requirement for man's character is that he *"be holy as He is holy."* It therefore follows that for the holy there can be only one end and that is heaven, and for entrance into heaven there is only one qualification, and that is holiness of heart and life. This is the one quality that has been consistent and constant throughout God's plan in creation and redemption. Holiness was the one true and essential requirement of God before man disobeyed and forfeited his holy estate.

Bishop Foster said, "In the University of Heaven, whose president is God, and whose catalog is the Bible, the course of study is plainly laid out. We say without fear of successful contradiction that God's Word has majored on holiness! It breathes in the prophecy, thunders in the Law, murmurs in the narrative, whispers in the promises, supplicates in the prayers, sparkles in the poetry, resounds in the songs, speaks in the types, glows in the imagery, voices in the language and burns in the spirit of the whole scheme, from Alpha to Omega, from its beginning to its end. Holiness! Holiness needed, Holiness required, holiness offered, holiness attainable, holiness a present duty, a present privilege, a present enjoyment, is the progress and completeness of the Bible's wondrous theme. It is the truth glowing all over, welling all through revelation, the glorious truth which sparkles and whispers and sings and shouts in all its history and biography and poetry and prophecy and precept and promise and prayer, the great central truth of Christianity."[1]

In calling man back to himself and restoring him to his lost image, God establishes and requires conditions and expects man's obedient response to those conditions. Initially, man lost the moral state of holiness through unbelief and disobedience, and in order to be restored he must respond in obedient faith. The work of the Holy Spirit is to convict man *of sin, because they* ***believe not on me*** (John 16:9). The plan of salvation, in each of its stages, has conditions that demand a response from man. For example, in order to be forgiven and regenerated man must repent and believe. In order for a believer to be sanctified wholly he must make a full and complete consecration and by faith receive the cleansing work of the Holy Spirit. In the progression of his Christian walk, he must willingly and joyfully continue, moment by moment, to hunger after and follow His Father's will and desire for his life.

Holiness was God's standard before the fall and naturally before any of the conditions for salvation was necessary. Following man's fall the plan of salvation was unfolded and the conditions were, and even now, are necessary for man's obedient response. God requires that sinners repent and confess, and He requires that believers crucify the self-life and consecrate their renewed selves to Him. The highest standard of life in this present world is exemplified in the holy character and righteous conduct of the Christian. Holiness is the only part of the entire Christian system that will exist beyond the grave. The time will come when there will be no need of repentance, confession, consecration, crucifixion, and such like, but *"without holiness no man shall see the Lord."* Holiness will be the climate of heaven and it will be the song of the redeemed throughout eternity.

In 1Thessalonians 4:1-8, Paul urged his brethren in Christ to abound in a pleasing walk before God by abstaining from evil passions. He told them that sanctification was God's will for them. *"For God hath not called us unto uncleanness, but unto holiness."* Here he places *uncleanness* as the antithesis to *holiness.* Then, with a bit of a warning, he says, *"He therefore that despiseth [rejects], despiseth [rejects] not man, but God, who hath also given us His Holy Spirit."* The warning is clear that whatever estimate one places on the call of God to holiness is likewise the estimate one places on God who gives the call. God's call to holiness is not an obscure, unimportant call, but is central and essential to the whole redemptive scheme, and we must consider it as imperative and not optional.

Holiness is likeness to God or Christ-likeness. Holiness in man involves separation from sin and total abandonment and devotion to God. It is God's _will_ for man (1 Thessalonians 4:3), it is God's _call_ to man (1 Thessalonians 4:7; 1 Peter 1:15), it is God's _choice_ for man (Ephesians 1:4; 2 Thessalonians 2:13). God's will for man is also His enablement, for He is El Shaddai (the all-sufficient God). God admonished Abram, *"Walk before me, and be thou perfect."* His admonition was supported by His adequacy as He identified himself as El Shaddai—the Almighty God (Genesis 17:1). Holiness is required by God's holy law, and His law never requires anything impossible, unreasonable or unnecessary. Holiness in man is derived from God and is attainable, relative, conditional and forfeitable.

Holiness in man is not absolute—only God is absolutely holy. It is not the state of holiness that Adam possessed before the fall and before sin's consequences. It is not angelic perfection, as that relates only to un-fallen angels. It is not a perfection of finality, as there is much growth and maturity to follow, and the holiness of man is not that which is yet to come in his glorified state, following his resurrection, when he will be delivered from the scars and presence of sin.

We understand that God takes the initiative by drawing man to Himself. Jesus said, *"I am the way, the truth, and the life: no man cometh unto the Father, but by me"* (John 14:6). From the very moment that man responded to that initial call of God in conviction, until he has safely entered into the eternal presence of God, it has been a perpetual walk in holiness. Let us examine a bit of the journey that brings us back to his full and final restoration.

1. **R. S. Foster,** *Christian Purity or The Heritage of Faith,* pp. 131, 132

V.

HOLINESS: THE FIRST WORK OF GRACE

As we have already noted, sin is two-fold in its nature. It is first an act of transgression that requires forgiveness because it produces guilt in the one who commits it. A sinful act involves man's volition for which he is responsible and accountable. It is an act of his will and will manifest itself in his outward conduct. Secondly, sin is an inner condition of the heart and is not related to his personal volition. It does not produce guilt, because one is not responsible for this pollution in the heart because it was inherited from our first parents in the fall. Therefore this inward pollution requires, not forgiveness, but cleansing.

In order for one to be delivered from all sin and be filled and fully possessed by the Holy Spirit, both forgiveness and cleansing must be experienced. God has provided both reconciliation and entire sanctification through His Son. Jesus, as Redeemer, made provisions to remove the sinner's guilt by His pardoning grace. He also made provision to remove the believer's pollution by His purifying grace. In the first work of grace one is born of the Spirit, and in the second he is baptized with the Spirit.

Let us examine the first work of grace, namely regeneration. The word "regenerate" means to "create anew." It takes place by the "quickening" work of the Holy Spirit. *"You hath He quickened, who were dead in trespasses and sins"* (Ephesians 2:1). This is an instantaneous work of grace and takes place in a crisis moment. The word "crisis" means "a crucial or decisive point or situation; a sudden change in the course of an acute disease which will determine recovery or death." Spiritually speaking, it is a point in time when one is suddenly brought from spiritual darkness into light and from spiritual death into life. He is born-again, or "born from above" by the Holy Spirit.

Jesus supplies a clear and concise meaning of the word "regeneration" in John 3:1-8. Here we have a dialog that takes place between Jesus and the inquiring Nicodemus. Nicodemus willingly acknowledged Jesus as Rabbi (teacher), but Jesus knew that he needed to know Him not merely as an instructor or teacher but that he needed to recognize Him as the Redeemer. Jesus, the greatest teacher the world has ever known, gave Nicodemus the greatest lesson of his life when he said to him, "*Ye must be born again*" (John 3:7). This is the first work of grace on one's journey to heaven.

1. Antecedents to the First Work of Grace

(a.) **Conviction** is the work of the Holy Spirit by which a man becomes convinced of his lost estate. It is often referred to as prevenient grace because God always takes the initiative in drawing sinners to Himself. Jesus said, "*No man can come to me, except the Father which hath sent me draw him: and I will raise him up at the last day*" (John 6:44). God is always previous in man's salvation because the Holy Spirit has come initially to "*reprove* (convince) *the world of sin...*" (John 16:8). This office work of the Holy Spirit arraigns man before the bar of his own conscience, making him aware of his guilty and condemned state, and causing him to realize his lost condition. This is what D. L. Moody was referring to when he said that you will never get

X

a man saved until first you get him lost. This is demon-
strated in the case of Saul on the road to Damascus. When
his heart was pricked by the Holy Spirit, he cried, *"Lord,
what will thou have me to do?"* (Acts 9:6). Sinners will not
seek forgiveness of their sins until God makes them aware
of their need of forgiveness. When man finally realizes his
need of seeking the Savior, it is not long until he discovers
that it was because the Savior had all of the time been seeking him. He is the "Seeking Savior."

(b.) Repentance is the next step in man's pursuit of
forgiveness. Repentance is defined as a change of mind, and
a change of direction, because saving faith cannot exist
while one's back is turned toward God. Repentance brings
one to an about-face turn toward God, and causes one to
"have another mind." Repentance will result in a sense of
shame and remorse, but it must involve something more.
There must be a *"godly sorrow"* that *"worketh repentance to
salvation not to be repented of"* (2 Corinthians 7:10).

Paul S. Rees affirmed that "Repentance is real when it
passes beyond grief to God, when it passes beyond sorrow to
surrender, and when it passes beyond failure to faith. The
conviction of sin and the shame it evokes must lead one to
action. It was when the Prodigal Son realized the shame of
the swine pen that he deliberately and decisively
announced, 'I will arise and go to my father!' Jesus added,
'He arose and went.'[1] Repentance is a knowledge of sin's
guilt, a sorrow for sin's act, an abandonment of sin's way,
and as God would lead and is possible, a correcting of sin's
wrongs (restitutions).

(c.) Faith is necessary and becomes active only when
repentance is genuine. As Paul taught, salvation is appro-
priated by *"repentance toward God, and faith toward our
Lord Jesus Christ"* (Acts 20:21). Richard S. Taylor wrote
that Biblical theology increasingly confirms the basic

34

insights of John Wesley, including his lifelong insistence that Christ died for man's sanctifying as well as justifying, that God's processes include a second definite work of grace, and that love is the universal evidence of one's inward holiness. "Our main doctrines," he said, "are **repentance, faith,** and **holiness**. The first of these we account, as it were, the porch of religion; the next, the door; the third, religion itself." Taylor further stated that if holiness is religion itself (in the Christian sense), no theology can be sound which treats it as an attic, or which makes either repentance or faith the house.[2] Faith is the door through which we must pass to enter the house of holiness. Faith is not only mental assent; it requires moral action. Our faith rests on the final word of Christ and the finished work of Calvary. What Jesus promised in His word has been provided on the cross.

There are four elements to evangelical faith. The first is knowledge (Romans 10:14), for man must have knowledge or light on something before he can believe in it. God's word supplies the facts on which our faith rests. Then secondly, assent must be given to the truthfulness of the fact. Thirdly, one must give the consent of his will to the facts known and assented to. Finally, one must appropriate—lay hold of— the truth known and assented to. To what truth asserts and demands, we consent, so that the truth may be experienced by our seeking souls.

2. Effects of the First Work of Grace

Justification is the judicial aspect of salvation. Through forgiveness, the penitent is made acceptable in a (legal relationship) with God, bringing him into harmony with the law of God. *"Being justified by faith, we have peace with God through our Lord Jesus Christ"* (Romans 5:1, 9,

16). Through repentance and faith one has been acquitted before the bar of justice of all of his crimes against the government of God. As far as possible and as God would lead, an honest effort must be made to rectify the wrongs committed against his fellow man (Luke 19:8). One must place his full reliance on the blood of Christ (Romans 3:25-26).

Regeneration, as has already been stated, means that spiritual life has been imparted, and fellowship is restored. This is known as the (parental aspect) of this work of grace. The believer is "begotten again" by an act of divine grace and power, and receives spiritual life (1 Peter 1:23). Fallen nature is renewed, resulting in what Chalmers called "the expulsive power of a new affection." The affections and allegiance of the heart have made a tremendous reversal. Many things that once were loved are now abhorred and have been replaced by those things that please God. We now love what He loves and hate what He hates.

Adoption is the (family aspect) of this new life experience. Once children of the devil, we are now transformed into sons of God (1 John 3:1). Though we once belonged to God through creation, Satan kidnapped us. Christ came into the world and paid the ransom necessary to restore us to God's family (Matthew 20:28). The Holy Spirit bears witness to the believing soul of this paternity (Romans 8:16; Galatians 4:6), and His witness is the birth certificate of the soul.

Thomas N. Ralston put it this way: "Justification removes our guilt, which is a barrier in the way of our admission into God's family; regeneration changes our hearts, imparting a fitness for admission into the family; and adoption actually receives us therein, recognizing us as God's children redeemed by Christ, washed and sanctified by His blood and Spirit, and admitted into covenant relation with God as our Father."[3]

There are those who teach that all human creatures are God's children. The Bible does not teach universal brotherhood or that God is a universal Father. It teaches that we all belong to God by creation, but we become children of God by way of adoption. In order to be adopted we are admonished to *"come out from among them, and be ye separate, saith the Lord, and touch not the unclean thing; and I will receive you, and will be a Father unto you, and ye shall be my sons and daughters, saith the Lord Almighty"* (2 Corinthians 6:17-18). *"as many as received him, to them gave he power to become sons of God"* (John 1:12).

This first work of grace is a marvelous experience that initiates one into a wonderful relationship with God. God has lifted the guilt from the penitent's heart and has given him a blood-bought pardon. There are distinguishing characteristics of this first work of grace.

First of all, one who has been regenerated (born-again) enjoys victory over outward and inward sin (1 John 3:8, 9, & 10). Christianity is the only religion that does not merely try to make a bad man better by rules and regulations. Through the work of God in regeneration it transforms a man from *spiritual death* into one that is *alive unto God*. Through God's quickening Spirit, the man once dead now has new life in Christ. Reformation cannot produce such a change in man. Reformation affects only the life that lies, as yet, in the future, but God's transforming work of grace forgives the sins of the past and enables him to conform to all the requirements of God's holy law in his deportment, and also he is enabled to control the unholy tendencies of a yet unsanctified heart.

Secondly, he not only has victory over sin but also victory over the world (1 John 5:4-5). The spirit and standards of the world no longer have power over him. Jesus said of His disciples, *"They are not of the world, even as I am not of* *the world"* (John 17:16). John said of believers, "The world knows them not because it knew him [Jesus] not" (I John 3:1). When one is born again he becomes a citizen of another and *"better country"* (Hebrews 11:16).

Thirdly, righteousness characterizes the regenerate life. The born-again lives in harmony with God, and as much as lies within them, they live at peace with men. They recognize that they are not possessors or owners of anything, but rather have been made stewards of all that God has blessed them with. They do not rob God or take advantage of their fellowmen.

The new Christian loves the truth and is loyal to the doctrines of God's word. He is always teachable because he knows that truth is progressive. Once he has received Christ as his Savior, his greatest desire is to be pleasing to the one to whom he owes his forgiveness. He is open and receptive to the Spirit's searching of his heart and life, and he is instant in his obedience to the Spirit's call or chastening.

In his classic, *New Testament Holiness*, Thomas Cook nicely sums up the regenerate experience. "Regeneration is holiness begun. Whatever is of the essence of holiness is found in germ in all who are children of God. Though all the elements of holiness are imparted, the work of inward renewal is only begun, not finished, by regeneration. On this point there is harmony of faith among all churches. They hold that regeneration does not free the soul from depravity. It checks the out-breaking of depravity into actual sin, but inward corruption remains, manifesting itself in a bias toward evil, in inclinations to sin, in a proneness to depart from God, 'a bent to sinning'.... In regeneration sin is subdued and conquered, but it is not destroyed. Depravity is suspended, held in check, repressed; but it is not fully expelled from the soul. It does not reign but it does exist.... There is an inner warfare in which flesh and spirit antagonize each other.... This infection of nature does remain, warring against the Spirit even in those who are regenerate. The result often is that from the germ-sins in the heart spring actual sins in the life."[4]

This first work of grace is a marvelous and complete work of God in man. Nothing is gained by minimizing the first work of grace in order to exalt the second. Both experiences are unique and complete works of the Holy Spirit in man. It does not take the second work of grace to make us victors over sin, as the minimum of salvation is salvation from sinning. *"Whosoever is born of God doth not commit sin"* (I John 3:9). However, the experience of entire sanctification makes victory easier and some cases more constant. It is therefore essential to *go on unto perfection* and be *sanctified wholly* in order to complete the work of purification and renovation that was begun in regeneration.

John Wesley said: "From long experience and observation, I am inclined to think, that whoever finds redemption in the blood of Jesus, whoever is justified, has then the choice of walking in the higher or lower path. I believe the Holy Spirit at that time sets before him "the more excellent way," and incites him to walk therein; to choose the narrowest path in the narrow way; to aspire after the heights and depths of holiness—after the entire image of God."[5]

Charles Spurgeon said, "There is a point of grace as much above the ordinary Christian as the ordinary Christian is above the world."[6] We ought to proclaim and most importantly exemplify holiness, the second work of grace, namely entire sanctification, in such a way that people will desire to experience the grace and live the life because of its inherent attractiveness. It is a beautiful and harmonious life to live and enjoy in this present world, and it holds out the hope of a life of eternal bliss with our Savior and the saints of all ages.

Here is wise counsel from R. S. Foster: "The truth to be preserved is that there is a higher experience possible to Christians than that which is attained in and at the time of regeneration; This must be so taught as not to reflect discredit on regeneration on the one hand or excite fanaticism on the other hand, and so as to inspire aspiration after it as a duty and privilege."[7]

1. **Paul S. Rees**, *Sermon in Heart and Life*, February 1952.

2. **Richard S. Taylor**, *Preaching Holiness Today*, p. 203.

3. **Thomas N. Ralston**, *Elements of Divinity*, pp. 435-436

4. **Thomas Cook**, *New Testament Holiness*, pp. 27-29

5. **John Wesley**, *Sermon LXXXIX, The More Excellent Way, No. 6*

6. **Thomas Cook**, *New Testament Holiness,* opening sentence in the book

7. **R. S. Foster,** *The Philosophy of Christian Experience*, pp. 159-160

VI.

HOLINESS: THE SECOND WORK OF GRACE

It is at this point in God's great plan of salvation that there has been so much controversy, even within the ranks of the Christian church, as to whether or not God is able to deliver man from all sin in this life. If He can deliver us from all sin in this life, then why does it require two works of grace to accomplish it? Perhaps the real dispute is not so much the "*addition*" of a second work of grace as it is with the "*subtraction*" of sin from the heart. It needs to be noted from the beginning, that it is, obviously, not a lack or weakness on God's part. When Jesus died on the cross and rose on the third day, the provisions that were needed for full deliverance from sin was complete. He accomplished, provisionally and potentially, in that moment, everything man needed. However, the provisions of Calvary must be actualized by faith in each person's heart.

The reasons for two works of grace are: 1. because sin is twofold in its nature, 2. because of the different requirements necessary to receive the benefits of the provisions of the cross. The requirements for a sinner to experience regeneration are repentance and faith, but the requirements for the believer to be wholly sanctified is to present himself a living sacrifice (consecration) and faith. The latter, *consecration*, cannot be executed until one is regenerated and has passed from death unto life. Man is unable to

42

exercise faith for two different things at one and the same time.

Those who oppose holiness may be said to do so from one of three causes: ignorance, prejudice, or unbelief. If they oppose it out of <u>ignorance</u>, they need to be instructed as to what sin is and does, and as to what holiness is and does. If they oppose it out of <u>prejudice</u> against it by reason of some inconsistent professor of the experience, or someone who wrested the Scriptures so as to teach what God never intended, they need to be persuaded by positive proof and consistent demonstration of the life of holiness. If they oppose holiness out of <u>unbelief</u>, it is proof that they *"love darkness rather than light, because their deeds are evil."* Such objectors need to be convicted by the power of the Holy Spirit as to the exceeding sinfulness of sin and the beauty of true holiness."[1]

(Italics and underlining are mine).

With this in mind we will now proceed on the topic entire sanctification, the central purpose of the writing of this book, but more importantly we believe it to be the central purpose of God's redemptive scheme.

1. **Roy S. Nicholson**, *True Holiness,* pp. 16-17

VII.

THE IMPORTANCE OF ENTIRE SANCTIFICATION

The greatest thing that can ever happen in the life of the Christian is for him to be sanctified wholly. This statement in no way casts aspersions on the work of regeneration; the greatest thing that can happen to a sinner is to be born again. Both works are a completed part in the whole scheme of full salvation. We are now speaking of the second work of grace, entire sanctification, and its importance in the life of the Christian. Entire sanctification as a second work of grace is a fact or it is not a fact. If it is true, (and it is true), then its importance cannot be overemphasized. As great and essential as regeneration is, there remains within man's heart a sin problem that, as of yet, has not been resolved. It is a moral condition that pardon cannot reach.

Sinful man lives under a dual sentence of death because of the twofold nature of sin. To illustrate this fact allow me to give a hypothetical example. A man commits a terrible crime and is tried and found guilty by a jury of his peers and is sentenced to be put to death. While awaiting his execution for the crime that he has committed he becomes very ill. The doctor examines the patient and discovers that he has a terminal disease. This man now faces death, not only for his crimes that he has committed but also because of the disease that he has been diagnosed with. If he is to live he must receive a pardon for his crime so that he doesn't suffer the legal penalty of death, but also he needs a cure from his disease that is eating at the vitals of his life.

So it is with every sinner. He must not only receive a pardon for his transgressions, he also needs the blood to purify his heart from this malady of the soul. It is this corrupt nature that every man inherited as a result of the fall of our first parents in the Garden. It is the depraved disposition behind every evil act that is committed. In the atonement Jesus provided, not only for the sinner, that he might believe and not perish, (John 3:16) but also for the Christian, that he might be sanctified wholly, (Ephesians 5:25-26).

Having illustrated the need of an unsanctified heart to be "entirely" sanctified, I want to define and give the meaning of sanctification. In a very real sense, every Christian is initially sanctified. In I Corinthians 1:30, the Apostle Paul addresses those who are in Christ as being sanctified. However, he writes in the third chapter that the brethren were yet *babes in Christ* and that they were demonstrating a very *carnal* disposition. He identifies the inward stirrings of *envy, strife, and divisions*. He made it clear that this is not the way the *spiritual man* lives. He, in essence, is saying that carnality is not the standard of Christianity but rather, holiness is the standard. Why else would he say, "*For ye are YET carnal...*"? He is implying that they needed to go on unto holiness so that they would not have these carnal tendencies. It is much like the admonition given by the writer of the Hebrew letter in chapter 5 and 6. They had lingered too long in the first stages of the "*first principles of the oracles of God; and have become such as have need of milk, and not of strong meat...*" While they should have become teachers they were yet as students having to be taught. They were admonished to "*leave the principles of the doctrine of Christ, let us go on unto perfection.*"

The writer remembers many years ago sharing the pulpit with one of the great men of the holiness movement, Dr. Ralph Earle. He taught that everyone is living either a fractured life, a fractional life, or a fulfilled life. He explained the fractured life as that of a sinner, he reminded us that the origin of the fraction came as a result of the fall of man. He said that the fractional life is one who has been regenerated but not yet entirely sanctified. He further stated that man is fulfilled when He is filled full with the Holy Spirit, *"ye are complete in Christ"* (Colossians 2:10). He stated that those who are living a fractional life should quickly seek and find the harmonizing experience of entire sanctification. If they linger too long in this stage of their Christian life, they will become a prey for the enemies' attacks and face the possibility of falling from grace.

When the Apostle Paul was writing his first epistle to the brethren of Thessalonica, he commended them and recounted their spiritual credentials as believers in the first chapter. As one reads this chapter he has to be impressed with these who live such exemplary Christian lives. However, when one reads the third chapter, he begins to sense Paul's burden for their spiritual welfare and his grave concern for the perfecting of their faith in order that their hearts might be established *"unblamable in holiness."* It was to this end that he was praying night and day. He was writing to admonish them to go on unto holiness (sanctification), and this, of itself, involves so true and so great a state of sanctification as to make this enlarging, qualifying or amplifying word **"*WHOLLY,*"** (I Thessalonians 5:23) necessary in justice to their already very blessed state of sanctification.

I share this account of the Thessalonians to show that the basal fact in sanctification is cleansing. This cannot be too strongly emphasized. The whole matter of salvation, in its three great epochs, has to do with man's sin problem. There is justification, with its guilt; sanctification with its corruption; and glorification with its consequences. Whatever other benefits are derived from these various epochs, these are fundamental. Justification and Entire Sanctification are the foundational works of grace upon which a Christian builds his life in this world.

J. Paul Taylor writes: "It is often assumed that justification is the foundation, while holiness of heart is the superstructure at which one works as long as he lives. On the contrary, entire holiness is part of the foundation. It is the top layer of stones, finishing the foundation…. When sanctification is 'entire,' the foundation is completed." He went on to say, "When this doctrine is not preached clearly and with power, people do not hunger for the experience. If they do not hunger for it intensely, they will not seek it. If they do not seek it, they will not find it. If they do not find it, they will not witness to it. Out of the church where this fatal lack occurs, one or more persons may enter the ministry. Not being in possession of the joyful experience, they will fail to preach it with assurance, and the vicious cycle begins once more to do its devastating work on the spiritual life of the church."[1]

✓ ## The Meaning of Sanctification

Webster's Dictionary

Sanctify: "1. To make sacred or holy, to set apart to a holy or religious use, to consecrate by appropriate rites, to hallow…. 2. To make free from sin, to cleanse from moral corruption and pollution. John 17:17, Esp. (Theol.) the act of God's grace by which the affections of men are purified or alienated from sin and the world, and exalted to a supreme love to God."

Century Dictionary

Sanctify: "To make holy or clean, either ceremonially or morally or spiritually; to purify or free from sin. In theology, the act of God's grace by which the affections of men are purified and the soul is cleansed from sin and consecrated to God; conformity of the heart and life to the will of God."

Standard Dictionary

Sanctify: "To make holy, render sacred or morally or spiritually pure; cleansed from sin; sanctification; specifically in theology, the gracious work of the Holy Spirit whereby the believer is freed from sin and exalted to holiness of heart and life."

Church of the Nazarene Manual

Entire Sanctification: "We believe that entire sanctification is that act of God, by which believers are made free from original sin, or depravity, and brought into a state of entire devotement to God, and the holy obedience of love made perfect.

It is wrought by the baptism with the Holy Spirit, and comprehends in one experience the cleansing of the heart from sin and the abiding, and indwelling presence of the Holy Spirit, empowering the believer for life and service.

Entire sanctification is provided by the blood of Jesus, is wrought instantaneously by faith, preceded by entire consecration; and to this work and state of grace the Holy Spirit bears witness.

This experience is also known by various terms representing its different phases, such as "Christian perfection," "perfect love," "heart purity," "the baptism with the Holy Spirit," "the fullness of the blessing," and "Christian holiness."

Wesleyan Methodist Church

Entire sanctification: "Entire sanctification is that work of the Holy Spirit by which the child of God is cleansed from all inbred sin through faith in Jesus Christ. It is subsequent to regeneration, and is wrought when the believer presents himself a living sacrifice, holy, and acceptable to God, and is thus enabled through grace to love God with all the heart and to walk in His holy commandments blameless."

Many years ago the Wesleyan Methodist Church adopted an "Interpretation" of this doctrine as "Appendix A," "The Reaffirmation of the Doctrines of Our Faith":

"We reaffirm our faith in the doctrine of entire sanctification, by which work of grace the heart is cleansed by the Holy Spirit from all inbred sin through faith in Jesus Christ when the believer presents himself a living sacrifice, holy and acceptable unto God, and is enabled, through grace, to love God with all his heart and to walk in His holy commandments blameless. By the act of cleansing, it is to be interpreted and taught by the ministry and teachers that it is not a "suppression" or a "counteraction" of "inbred sin" so as to "make it inoperative," but "to destroy" or "to eradicate" from the heart so that the believer not only has a right to heaven, but is so conformed to God's nature that he will enjoy God and heaven forever. These terms are what we hold that cleansing from all sin implies."

1. **J. Paul Taylor**, *Holiness The Finished Foundation,* pp. 9-10

VIII.

REASONS WE HOLD TO THE TRUTH OF ENTIRE SANCTIFICATION

The first reason is that it is a scriptural doctrine. Nothing is clearer from the teachings of the entire Bible, than that God is a holy Being. This being true He could never approve or accept, into His fellowship, an unholy creature. He is light to the exclusion of all darkness, He is love and will not permit carnal hatred into His economy, He is holy and will not allow sin in His presence, and He is sovereign and will not tolerate any rebellion. Sin is the antithesis of holiness and the twain shall never meet.

In the study of comparative religions we discover that men tend to become like the gods that they serve. If they serve a vulgar or lustful god, a low standard of morality will characterize their lives. If their god is tyrannical and a despot, then a warlike spirit will characterize their lives, etc. The true and living God is holy. His holy nature becomes the standard for His people. This is why Peter gave the command, *"But as he which hath called you is holy, so be ye holy in all manner of conversation."* (I Peter 1:15). "God is love" (*agape*, holy, selfgiving) (I John 4:8), and the only thing that can satisfy love is love. When one reads the Holy Scriptures he discovers that it is the greatest love story that was ever told.

The second reason is because it is a <u>desirable doctrine</u>. I recall while growing up in a small community as a young lad that I was privileged to attend a little Methodist church. Those who taught me the story of Jesus were godly people. The ones that I vividly recall were two ladies, Miss Jean Holt and Mrs. Gorman. They will never know the impact that they made in my young and impressionable mind. They were Sunday school teachers, and they faithfully served Jesus every day. I got a revelation of the Savior by watching their lives. I'm sorry that I never became a Christian at that time, but their influence was the initial dynamic through which I would later turn to Christ.

We moved from that small community when I was about 14 years of age to another small community. It was here, through the tragic loss of a five-year-old sister, that I for the first time came face to face with the reality and finality of death. The days following that tragedy were very dark and grievous, but it occasioned an opportunity for God to show me my spiritual need. He sent special people into my life that would teach me the way of holiness by word and deed. It was in a country Church of the Nazarene that I found Jesus as my Savior.

It was the beauty of Christian holiness displayed in the lives of these people that moved me to the Christ. I have looked back across the years of my life and realized that He was always faithful to use His children to reveal Himself to me, even when I did not respond as I should have. I have been so thankful for His patience and mercy, for no one needed it more than I did, and still do. I met my wife in that little church, and God has blessed our marriage and family beyond description.

It was just a few weeks following my conversion that I was made to realize a deeper need in my heart that forgiveness had not afforded me. I could not have expressed it in these terms at the time of my new life in Christ, but I will try to state now, how I felt back then. God had performed a wonderful and beautiful work when He transformed my life and made me a new creature. My rationale was that if He could do that, He must also have the power to complete the work in my heart that as of yet was unfinished. I knew that there had to be provisions in the atonement to not only reach the height of His demand on my life but also the depth of my hunger. I was not driven to be sanctified wholly, but I was drawn by the attractiveness of the life that I had seen displayed in the lives of other sanctified Christians. Paul admonished Titus to teach the Christians to live their lives *"that they may adorn the doctrine of God our Savior in all things."* (Titus 2:10). In other words he was saying that we must live the Christian life so that our lives will beautify the Gospel of Christ. It is thus that men and women will be drawn to Him. I know for I'm a happy beneficiary of this truism.

Holiness is beautiful and desirous in spite of its enemies' efforts to discredit it. Holiness is also beautiful in spite of its friends who unwittingly misrepresent it. Much is done by enemies of holiness to discount its qualities. Also, much is done in the name of holiness which is not consistent with the qualities of godliness, and therefore, is not **true holiness.**

The third reason that we gladly hold to this truth is because it is the necessary qualification and equipment for successful soul winning. After Jesus had given the Great Commission to His disciples, He commanded them to tarry in Jerusalem until they were endued with power from on high. This was the necessary equipment that was needed to accomplish His continued work on earth. When the Holy Spirit came upon them at Pentecost, they were not only cleansed from sin, but so filled with divine love that they eagerly sought the salvation of men.

Some months ago I was told of a man who had a rather minor surgery. Ordinarily it would require only a day or two in the hospital, and then he would be released to continue to live a normal life. However, the following day the man grew worse, and in just a matter of days he expired. When they determined the cause of death they discovered that the surgical tools that were used on him during the surgery were not clean and caused a staph infection that proved to be fatal.

It is the Christian's responsibility, as well as privilege, to minister to the sin sick soul. However, we must not touch the festering sores of the sins of others until our hands and hearts are clean lest we cause harm and hurt to those to whom we minister. Jesus knew that the disciples were not qualified or equipped to minister to the needs of others without the cleansing or sanctifying work of the Holy Spirit. On the Day of Pentecost they experienced the purifying of their hearts, and they were endued with power sufficient for the task.

The fourth reason we hold so dear to the truth of entire sanctification is that it is the passport to heaven. Hebrews 12:14 says, *"Follow peace with all men, and holiness, without which no man shall see the Lord." Jesus teaches in the Sermon on the Mount that the pure in heart shall see the Lord* (Matthew 5:8).

There have been times that we travel from one nation to another. Before we are able to enter other nations there are certain restrictions and requirements. We must have an up-to-date passport. Certain nations require that we have a visa, and in some areas we must have certain inoculations in order not to spread or be inflicted by diseases. If one does not adhere to these rules, and other restrictions, he will not be permitted to enter the country. The reason is because they are sovereign nations, and they have the right to set the standard by which anyone enters their country.

God is sovereign of the universe, and He sets the standard necessary for one to enter heaven, and that standard is holiness. Heaven is a holy place where a holy God sits on His holy throne. Surrounding Him will be all the holy saints and holy angels of all the ages, and together they will be singing the anthem, holy, holy, holy is the Lord Almighty. Therefore it seems to me, in order to be consistent, if one desires to go to a holy heaven hereafter, he must have a desire to be holy in heart and life here and now.

Henry Clay Morrison wrote: "In the nature of things, there can be no heaven for an unholy soul. To be out of harmony with God, to love what He hates, and to hate what He loves, makes peace with God impossible and that which makes peace with God impossible makes heaven impossible.... The people should be taught everywhere that Jesus did not die so much to save them from hell or to save them in heaven; He died to save them from sin; salvation from sin makes hell an impossibility and heaven a certainty."[1] Holiness is the climate of heaven, and when one experiences the cleansing work of entire sanctification he enjoys a foretaste of heaven to come so that when he arrives on the heavenly shore he will not have to get used to the environment or adjust to the climate. Holiness is a bit of heaven that God puts within man as he makes his pilgrimage to his celestial home.

"Since God is infinite in holiness and since His holiness in its quality and content clothes Him in an unspeakable and unapproachable glory, it takes this quality of character in every moral being to satisfy God. When this moral state is realized in human experience, the barriers to our fellowship and union with God are removed. The basis of eternal felicity is secured. It takes this experience not only to satisfy God, but to fully and permanently satisfy man. We were created with capacity for this very objective. Man will never be satisfied outside of the orbit of God's perfect will in which he possesses the moral quality of character which holiness represents. The most terrifying picture of eternal damnation in the written Word is the eternal unrest of a lost soul.

"Man in final separation from God will find himself in a state of hopeless despair and of eternal moral darkness with nothing to satisfy the deep of his own nature. Hell will be eternal unrest with no place for the soul of man's foot to rest for a single second. It will be despair without hope, darkness without light, and sorrow without any alleviation of even temporary joy. It will be sin let loose on itself without any of the mollifying influences of the presence of righteousness.

"The exact opposite of this is the thing for which God created us and for which He bled and died to redeem us. Heaven represents to us eternal rest; not the rest of inactivity, but the rest of perfect harmony, the absence of all friction and care, the presence of fullness of joy. It will be light without darkness and joy unmingled with sorrow; yea, in the finality of redemption, which includes the glorification of our humanity, we shall be prepared to actually see and live in the presence of and share the eternal felicity and glory of our infinite Redeemer. Preparation as to moral quality of character for this great consummation of God's plan is to be made here and now. We are to be recovered to the moral likeness of God through the merit of the atoning sacrifice and by the agency of God, the Holy Spirit."[2]

I read the little booklet written by Dr. W. B. Godbey entitled, "Holiness or Hell." I realize that many are repulsed by such an assertion, but when reasoned logically it is a valid statement. The only reason for any one to be lost in hell is their lack of holiness. The only reason a soul is saved to heaven is holiness. There is not a holy person in hell, neither is there a sinner in heaven. Their respective rewards are determined by the law of God's will requiring holiness.

1. **Henry C. Morrison**, *Tarry Ye*, (The Fullness of Redemption), p. 7

2. **C. W. Butler**, *Faith Building Messages*, pp. 41-43

IX.

OLD TESTAMENT TYPES OF TWO WORKS OF GRACE

(1.) There were two crossings of the children of Israel on their journey to the land of Canaan: The crossing of the Red Sea and the crossing of the Jordan. The first crossing was when God led the children of Israel out of the land of Egypt. The armies of Pharaoh went in pursuit of the children of Israel to bring them back into captivity. They arrived at the banks of the Red Sea as their enemy was pressing down upon them. Moses seeks the wisdom and will of God, and God instructs him to raise the rod over the Red Sea, and the waters separate, and the wind dries the ground, and they cross over dry shod. When the Egyptians tried to cross the Red Sea, God closed the waters against them, and they drowned in the sea. This was the first deliverance which typified the work of regeneration, when a sinner flees to God for deliverance from the bondage of sin and its guilt. At this crossing God aided their faith by opening the waters before they stepped into the sea. They had their enemy pressing down upon them, and God made a way of escape. Their fear of being taken captive again and the awareness of a way of deliverance were helpful in their response.

Many years later, following their wilderness wanderings, they came to the Jordan. When they arrived at Jordan, there were no enemies pressing them to cross over. The river was at flood stage, and to step into the water was imminent death by drowning. However, God had directed

Joshua to let the Levites take the ark of the covenant into the midst of the Jordan, and the people would follow thereafter. While they were not driven by any enemies to cross over, they were being drawn by the blessings and privileges that were awaiting them in the land of Canaan. So fear was not the motivating factor, as in the crossing of the Red Sea, but the fruit and freedom of God's Promised Land was their motivation. So it is when one seeks to be entirely sanctified, not because of God's impending wrath but rather because of His impelling love. *"Faith's foot must walk the swelling flood and firmly claim the cleansing blood."*

(2.) This awakens us to the rest that God has promised to His people. Not all of the children of Israel that left Egypt entered the land of Canaan. Many who wandered in the wilderness for forty years did not live to experience and enjoy this rest of Canaan. They would not believe the promises of God and disobeyed His word and died in the wilderness. Canaan was to be the promised inheritance of God to His children. In Hebrews 3:15-19, *"While it is said, Today if ye will hear His voice, harden not your hearts, as in the provocation* (wilderness). *For some, when they had heard, did provoke: howbeit not all that came out of Egypt by Moses. But with whom was He grieved forty years? Was it not with them that had sinned, whose carcasses fell in the wilderness? And to whom sware He that they should not enter into His rest, but to them that believed not? So we see that they could not enter in because of unbelief."* Here the Apostle is revealing why many in the wilderness forfeited their inheritance, and it was through unbelief. It was one thing to be delivered from Egyptian bondage but quite another to enter into their promised land of Canaan, the land of rest. The hymn writer puts it very succinctly when he wrote:

"He brought me out, to bring me in,

Where shall I then His praise begin;

Freedom from sin, Canaan within,

He brought me out, to bring me in. "

As with the Israelites, God brings us out of the world of sin (Egypt) in order to bring us into a life of holiness (Canaan). When we read in Hebrews chapter 4, the writer starts this chapter with these words: *Let us therefore fear, lest, a promise being left us of entering into His rest, any of you should seem to come short of it.* " He further warns us in verse 6, *"They to whom it was first preached entered not in because of unbelief..."* and finally reminds us that *"There remaineth therefore a rest to the people of God."*

As Canaan was the inheritance of the Israelites, holiness (entire sanctification) is the inheritance of the saints. Holiness unclaimed is as unsatisfying as Canaan unpossessed. When we are regenerated by His Spirit we become joint heirs with Christ. We are told that, *"after that ye believed, ye were sealed with the Holy Spirit of promise, which is the earnest* (a sample and a surety of the final inheritance. The final inheritance is what Peter writes about in I Peter 1:4. An *'earnest'* is a <u>sample</u> of what is yet to come and a <u>surety</u> that it will be there when we come to receive it. It used to be that when one purchased a property that he was given a bag of the soil or ground that he had purchased and they called it an *'earnest.'* It was a sample of his purchase and the certainty that it would be his when he closed the deal.) *of our inheritance until the redemption of the purchased possession, unto the praise of His glory."*

It was included in the Apostle Paul's commission when he said that he was to preach *"forgiveness of sins and* **INHERITANCE** *among them which are sanctified by faith that is in me"* (Acts 26:18).

There are many other types that one could present such as:

(3.) The cleansing of the leper (Leviticus 14:8-9) and the two washings of the leprous garments (Leviticus 13:47-59).

(4.) The two rooms in the temple, the holy place and the holiest of all (Exodus 26:31-33)

(5.) The two types of service, a bond slave, the other a love slave (Exodus 21:1-6).

X.

OLD TESTAMENT EXAMPLES OF TWO WORKS OF GRACE

Jacob was one of the Old Testament patriarchs who had two very different and distinct experiences that typify two works of grace. After cheating his brother out of his paternal blessing and his rich prophetic inheritance, with the help of his mother he fled for his life. He went to Padanaram to work for his uncle Laban. The first night of his journey he had an encounter with God at the place called Luz. He dreamed of a ladder between heaven and earth on which angels descended and ascended. The Lord stood above the ladder, making rich promises to Jacob. On awakening he said, "*Surely the Lord is in this place; and I knew it not*" (Genesis 28:16). He renamed the place Bethel (house of God) and the stone on which he had pillowed his head became a pillar which he anointed with oil, signifying its dedication to the Lord. He also promised to give God a tithe of all that God gave to him. This marked an epoch in the life of Jacob which may properly stand for his conversion.

Twenty years later Jacob gathered up all of his possessions and his family and started on his journey toward Canaan, the land of his nativity. Following several significant events on his journey, he has another encounter with God at the brook Jabbok, which means "poured out." "*There wrestled a man with him*," either the pre-incarnate Christ or some other divine being. The struggle continued until the daybreak, and finally the heavenly wrestler threw

Jacob's hip out of joint. Jacob, no longer wrestling but clinging to him said, *"I will not let thee go, except thou bless me."* He was asked, *"What is thy name?"* His name denoted his character, and *"he said, Jacob."* Jacob means "supplanter" (deceiver). The wrestler replied, *"Thy name shall be called no more Jacob, but Israel: for as a prince thou hast power with God and with men, and hast prevailed"* (Genesis 32:24-31). This experience was a second epoch in the life of Jacob. He called this place Peniel, which means the (face of God). Once we have been to our Bethel, God will not leave us until we have been brought, in His providence, to the place that is called Peniel.

Isaiah has been called the "evangelical prophet" of the Old Testament. He prophesied more concerning the coming Messiah than any other prophet. He served during the reign of Uzziah the King of Judah. As long as Uzziah did right in the sight of the Lord the Kingdom prospered, but there came a time when the King transgressed against his God. *"But when he was strong, his heart was lifted up to his destruction: for he transgressed against the Lord to burn incense upon the altar of incense"* (II Chronicles 26:16). This was sacrilegious, disobedience to the commands of God, as only the priests were to minister in the temple. Because of his sin, Uzziah was stricken with leprosy and died later in isolation. Isaiah had been brought up in the king's court. He had been accustomed to looking to the king. But now the throne of Judah was vacant, and Isaiah was broken-hearted, and he went into the temple to pray. He soon discovered that though he lost an earthly king, while in the temple he received a vision of the eternal King, the King of kings.

Isaiah not only caught a glimpse of the Lord all-exalted, all-mighty, all-present, but he saw the Lord all-holy. The seraphims cried one to another and said, *"Holy, holy, holy is the Lord of hosts; the whole earth is full of His glory"* (Isaiah 6:3). It was as a result of that great vision, when Isaiah the prophet saw the *"Holy One of Israel,"* that he caught a glimpse of his own uncleanness and cried, *"Woe is me! For I am undone and ruined, because I am a man of unclean lips; for my eyes have seen the King, the Lord of hosts!"* He realized that just as Uzziah was a leper in the physical, he had a leprous heart.

Here was a young court preacher who had been Jehovah's servant for a number of years and now found himself in the throes of an advanced spiritual crisis. When he confessed that he was a man of unclean lips, he was simply confessing that he was a man with an impure heart. Immediately following his confession the angel of the Lord took a live coal from the altar, and touched his lips, and said, *"Thine iniquity is taken away, and thy sin purged"* (Isaiah 6:7). If Isaiah needed the cleansing fire to cleanse all impurities of his heart, each of us must experience the refining fire as well. May every believer pray:

"Oh, that in me the sacred fire
Might now begin to glow;
Burn up the dross of base desire,
And make the mountains flow."
"Thou, who at Pentecost did fall,
Do Thou my sin consume;
Come, Holy Ghost, for Thee I call;
Spirit of burning, come."
"Refining fire, go through my heart,
Illuminate my soul;
Scatter thy life through every part,
And sanctify the whole."

Charles Wesley

David is another person who was a recipient of two epochal works of grace. We see this truth revealed in the penitential prayer of David following his dreadful act of adultery with Bathsheba, and the subsequent murder of her husband, Uriah, along with his deceitful schemes of trying to cover up his sins. The prayer in Psalms 51 was born out of an acute consciousness of his sin, for he confesses in verse three, "*I acknowledge my transgressions: and my sin is ever before me.*" Here he identifies the dual nature of sin, one consisting of the acts of transgressions and the other being the sin principle. For the former, David prays for God's tender mercies to "*blot out my transgressions*" (v. 1), and for the latter, he prays, "*Wash me thoroughly from mine iniquity, and cleanse me from my sin*" (v. 2).

David knew that sin remained in him following the forgiveness of his transgressions. He believed that God could cleanse the depths of depravity that remained by the creative, cleansing ministry of the Holy Spirit, and he cries, "*Create in me a clean heart, O God*" (v. 10). He knew that the root had to be removed so that the symptoms would not appear. Therefore he prayed for God to purify the fountain so that the stream would be undefiled.

These are a few examples, but they are enough to show that two works of grace are threaded throughout the whole plan of God's redemptive scheme. From the fall of man in the Garden, examples throughout the entire Old Testament and as we will further see, examples throughout the entire New Testament, make this a central truth of God's Word.

XI.

NEW TESTAMENT EXAMPLES OF TWO WORKS OF GRACE

There are numerous examples in the New Testament of those who were believers and had a second crisis experience that resulted in the cleansing of the heart from depravity. We will endeavor to list a few examples.

The disciples are wonderful examples of this truth. That they received two works of grace cannot be disputed. They left all to follow Jesus and walked with Him for some three years. They watched Him as He fed the hungry, healed the sick, saved the lost, turned water into wine, raised the dead to life, cast out demons and many other miracles. They were students of His teaching ministry. They knew His purpose was to do the will of His heavenly Father; they were glad recipients of His promises, and the object of His prayers. As He came down to the end of His earthly life, He drew them off to Himself and delivered His last instructions to them. During the final week of His earthly life Jesus spent His time preparing the hearts of these disciples for the coming Holy Spirit. There are many evidences to substantiate that they were Bible Christians. We shall list a few of these evidences:

a. They were enjoying God's keeping grace: (John 17:12)

This chapter has been called the High Priestly Prayer. It is a record of Jesus praying and petitioning His Father. It has been stated that when one reads the Gospel of John, it is as though he is entering the tabernacle. As one reads the first 12 chapters it is as though he has entered the outer court of the tabernacle. Chapters 13-16 one has now entered into the holy place of the tabernacle, but when he embarks upon the 17th chapter, he needs to do so very reverently, as he is now approaching the inner sanctum, the Holy of holies, where Jesus is speaking to His Father. Of the disciples Jesus prays, *"While I was with them in the world, I kept them in thy name: those that thou gavest me I have kept, and none of them is lost, but the son of perdition, that the Scriptures might be fulfilled."* Several times the word *kept* or *keep* is used in this chapter and sometimes it means (outer) "protection" and sometimes it means (inner) "preservation."

b. They were not of this world: (John 17:14)

In this High Priestly prayer, as we continue to listen as Jesus petitions the Father, He does not pray for the world but for the disciples of His day and all who would follow, including even us. Of these disciples He prays that *"I have given them thy word; and the world hath hated them, because they were not of the world, even as I am not of the world"* (vs. 14). A good evidence that one belongs to Christ is that the world does not know nor fellowship with them because they have nothing in common with the world.

"For what fellowship hath righteousness with unrighteousness, and what communion hath light and darkness. And what concord hath Christ with Belial? Or what part hath he that believeth with an infidel. And what agreement hath the temple of God with idols? for ye are the temple of the living God; as God hath said, I will dwell in them, and walk in them; and I will be their God, and they shall be my people. Wherefore come out from among them, and be ye separate, saith the Lord, and touch not the unclean thing; and I will

receive you. And will be a Father unto you and ye shall be my sons and daughters, saith the Lord Almighty" (II Corinthians 6:14-18).

c. Their names were written in heaven: (Luke 10:20)

The disciples came to Jesus and were elated over the fact that "even the devils are subject unto us through thy name." (vs.1) Jesus was trying to enforce upon their minds that, whatever God is able to do through these infirm, human vessels, He (God) alone deserves the glory and that this was not to be their rejoicing point. If they are not careful this attitude can become an occasion for selfish pride. He says they should rejoice primarily that their names are written in heaven and because of Christ our Savior.

d. They were commissioned and sent by Jesus: (Luke 9:1-2)

There should be no questions in our minds that Jesus never commissioned a sinner to do His bidding. No one who has not received Christ, who is dead in their sins and dwells in darkness, could ever declare the message of the *Light of Life.* It would be a contradiction of the highest order. These disciples, with all of their faults and flaws, were nevertheless able to serve Christ and humanity because they were truly regenerated and effective disciples.

Having said all of that, there were still spiritual deficiencies that surfaced from time to time that required another and deeper work of grace. I will highlight a few of those times in the life of the disciples that exposes their spiritual infancy.

1. They displayed a revengeful spirit: (Luke 9:52-54)

It occurred when Jesus and the disciples came into a village of Samaritans, and they would not receive Jesus. This provoked the disciples, and when *"James and John saw this, they said, Lord, wilt thou that we command fire to come down from heaven, and consume them, even as Elijah did? But He turned, and rebuked them, and said, ye know not what manner of spirit ye are of. For the Son of man is not come to destroy men's lives, but to save them."* These disciples sought to destroy those who treated them despitefully, but that was not the spirit of the Constitution of the Kingdom. In the Sermon on the Mount, Jesus taught that they were to pray for them (Matthew 5:44).

2. Peter revealed a spirit of self-righteousness and arrogance: (Matthew 26:33-35)

When Jesus told them, within hours of His crucifixion, that they would smite the Shepherd, and the sheep would scatter abroad, Peter was quick to answer in his own defense and said, *"Though all men shall be offended because of thee, yet will I never be offended."* He later, when accused of being one of them, showed a cowardly spirit and denied the Lord three times as Jesus predicted he would.

3. They were selfishly struggling for position in the Kingdom: (Luke 9:46)

They had not learned the principle of the Kingdom that Jesus taught when He said in Matthew 18:4, *"Whosoever therefore shall humble himself as this little child, the same is greatest in the kingdom of heaven."*

4. They were looking for an earthly kingdom that they would rule: (Acts 1:6)

"When they therefore were come together, they asked of Him saying, Lord, wilt thou at this time restore again the kingdom to Israel? And He said unto them, it is not for you to know the times or the seasons, which the Father has put in His own power." Before Pentecost their concern was an

earthly kingdom, but on the eve of His ascension Jesus put away any question concerning the return of the scepter to Israel. He placed the emphasis on the pouring out of the Holy Spirit upon the believers. Following Pentecost the Apostles never allowed the matter of the coming age eclipse the emphasis that Jesus had placed upon the dispensation of the Holy Spirit and His sanctifying work. The following recounts the disciples second experience, as well as others.

(1.) On the Day of Pentecost when the disciples received ✓ the Promised Holy Spirit as a second work of grace, it wrought such a change in their lives that those looking on asked, *"What meaneth this?"* "Experientially, it meant that the disciples' hearts were purified by faith. Practically, it meant that the disciples had received the power of the Spirit to give and love and serve. Dispensationally, it meant that the Spirit of Christ, in fulfillment of promise, had come to superintend and extend the cause of Christ as started by Jesus in person. On the wings of the Spirit and through the lives of holy men and women, the Gospel of Christ was destined to be preached for a witness unto all creatures before His return."[1]

This experience came upon the disciples as a second and an instant epochal experience. They had already known Christ as their Savior as they walked with Him daily on this earth. It was not something they experienced by a growth process but quite the contrary, *"When the Day of Pentecost was fully come, they were all with one accord in one place. And suddenly there came a sound from heaven as of a rushing mighty wind, and it filled all the house where they were sitting. And there appeared unto them cloven tongues like as of fire, and it sat upon each of them. And they were all filled with the Holy Ghost"* (Acts 2:1- 4a).

(2.) Philip went down in Samaria to preach Christ to them and wrought many miracles before them, and many gladly received the Word of God and were saved and even baptized. When Jerusalem heard of the revival in Samaria they sent Peter and John down who laid hands on them, and they received the Holy Ghost (Acts 8:5-17). These were the same people that before Pentecost the disciples wanted to destroy by calling fire down from heaven. This certainly illustrates a drastic change had occurred in the hearts of the disciples and also that these Samaritans had received two works of grace. The first work of grace was when they believed and were baptized under Philip's ministry. The second was in response to the ministry of Peter and John.

(3.) We have already mentioned the conversion of Saul on the road to Damascus followed by his reception of the Holy Ghost when Ananias laid hands on him, and he received his sight (Acts 9:1-17).

(4.) The Christians in Corinth were babes in Christ. While babes they manifested traits of carnality. They were unable to eat the meat of the Word of God because of their spiritual infancy they could only take the milk of the Word. Their lives evidenced an envious spirit which produced strife and division. They had what some would call "preachers' religion" as each one had their favorite preacher which produced schisms in the church. Paul later led them into "*a more excellent way,*" revealed in I Corinthians 13, the way of perfect love, a deeper experience.

(5.) "*Paul passing through the upper coasts came to Ephesus: and finding certain disciples, he said unto them, have ye received the Holy Ghost since ye believed? And they said unto him, we have not so much as heard whether there be any Holy Ghost.*" They had received the baptism of repentance, (John baptized no one who did not give evidence of repentance, Matthew 3:7-8). "*And when Paul had laid his hands upon them, the Holy Ghost came on them...*" (Acts

19:1-6). This reception of the Holy Ghost was second and subsequent to what they had experienced before.

There are many other examples of those in the New Testament who experienced sanctification as a second work of grace, but these are sufficient to make our point.

Antecedents to the Second Work of Grace

(a.) Conviction for the need of a clean heart is an essential ingredient to motivate one to seek God. George Fox, the founder of the Society of the Friends, said that he recognized his need to be made pure in his heart, because there was something within that would not be patient, tender and kind. He sought the Lord, and he said that God took out those carnal stirrings, and then he "shut the door."

"A deep conviction that we are not yet whole; that our hearts are not fully purified; that there is yet in us a "carnal mind," which is still in its nature "enmity against God;" that a whole body of sin remains in our heart, weakened indeed, but not destroyed; shows, beyond all possibility of doubt, the absolute necessity of a further change. We allow, that at that very moment of justification, we are *born again*: in that instant we experience that inward change from "darkness into marvelous light;" from the image of the brute and the devil, into the image of God; from the earthly, sensual, devilish mind, to the mind which was in Christ Jesus. But are we then *entirely* changed? Are we *wholly* transformed into the image of Him that created us? Far from it: we still retain a depth of sin; and it is the consciousness of this which constrains us to groan, for full deliverance, to Him that is mighty to save. Hence it is those believers who are not convinced of the deep corruption of their hearts, or but slightly, and, as it were, notionally convinced, have little concern for *entire sanctification*. They may possibly hold the opinion, that such a thing is to be, either at death, or sometime they know not when, before it. But they have no great uneasiness for the want of it, and no great hunger and thirst after it. They cannot, until they know themselves better, until they repent in the sense above described, until God unveils the inbred monster's face, and shows them the real state of their souls. Then only, when they feel the burden, will they groan for deliverance from it. Then, and not til then, will they cry out, in the agony of their soul,

> *"Break off the yoke of inbred sin,*
> *And fully set my spirit free!*
> *I cannot rest till pure within,*
> *Till I am wholly lost in thee."[2]*

John Wesley speaks concerning the stirrings of carnality after conversion: "How naturally do those who experience such a change imagine that all sin is gone; that it is utterly rooted out of their hearts, and has no more any place therein! How easily do they draw that inference, *'I feel no sin; therefore, I have none: it does not stir; therefore, it does not exist: it has no motion; therefore, it has no being!'* But it is seldom long before they are undeceived, finding sin was only suspended, not destroyed. Temptation returns, and sin revives; showing it was only stunned before, not dead. They now feel two principles in themselves, plainly contrary to each other; *'the flesh lusting against the Spirit,'* nature opposing the grace of God. They cannot deny, that, although they still feel power to believe in Christ, and to love God; and although His 'Spirit' still 'witnesses with their spirit, they are children of God;' yet they feel in themselves sometimes pride or self-will, sometimes anger or unbelief. They find one or more of these frequently *stirring* in their hearts, though not *conquering;* yea, perhaps, thrusting sore at them that they may fall; but the Lord is their help."[3]

In addition to this conviction of the remains of sin in the believer, he must be fully persuaded that provisions have been made, in the atonement, for its cleansing. When those two things are acknowledged then the first and only business of the Christian is to diligently pursue a clean heart until it is experienced in the soul and witnessed to by the Spirit of holiness who does the work within. Jesus taught in the Sermon on the Mount, *"Blessed are they which do hunger and thirst after righteousness: for they shall be filled."* (Matthew 5:6).

The enemy will do his best to keep one from believing that it is possible to have a clean heart in this world. There will be many people who will try to dissuade one from seeking the experience and will even present questions and arguments against it being possible.

One must remember that this is the will of God (I Thessalonians 4:3 *"even your sanctification"*), the call of God (I Thessalonians 4:7 *"unto holinesss"*), and the choice of God for man (Ephesians 1:4 *"chosen us in Him that we should be holy"*). He who wills, calls, and has chosen us to be holy, has the power and adequacy to accomplish it in our hearts. We must desire and seek all that He has provided for us. Richard S. Taylor said, "The minimum measure of grace acceptable is an intense desire for the maximum measure of grace available."

Roy S. Nicholson writes, "As surely as one begins to teach the possibility of full salvation as a personal experience to be obtained in this life, he faces those who raise questions and interpose objections. One of the questions asked is: 'Can God sanctify the soul entirely in this life?' The answer is found in Paul's reference to the ability of God *"to do exceedingly abundantly above all that we ask or think, according to the power that worketh in us"* (Ephesians 3:20). Another question is: 'Will God entirely sanctify the soul in this life?' And again the scriptures replies: *'This is the will of God, even your sanctification…God hath not called us to uncleaness but unto holiness'* (I Thessalonians 4:3, 7). The *third question is:* 'Does God sanctify entirely, here and now? Once more the scripture gives the answer, when incident to Paul's prayer for the Thessalonians' entire sanctification and blameless preservation, he declares: *'Faithful is He that calleth you, who also will do it'* (I Thessalonians 5:23-24)."[4] (Underline and italics are mine)

For every God-given desire God has provided a corresponding satisfaction for the desire. For hunger there is food; for thirst there is water; for fellowship there are friends; etc. I recall that following my own conversion, like Wesley said, because I felt no stirrings of sin I assumed that it did not exist. I wanted only to be pleasing to my Savior, and as much as possible I wanted to reflect His image and likeness. However, it wasn't long before I was made conscious of something within that was very much unlike my Savior. I knew that His command was *"Be ye holy, for I am holy"* (I Peter 1:16). As I sought the cleansing of my heart, I did so believing that there must be grace enough to reach the height of His command and also the depth of my hunger, and indeed there was.

(b.) Consecration is the next requisite in our pursuit of holiness. The Apostle Paul exhorts, in Romans 12:1, *"I beseech you therefore, brethren, by the mercies of God, that ye present your bodies a living sacrifice, holy, acceptable unto God, which is your reasonable service."* This is an admonition given to the "brethren" and not to the sinner. Therefore one must have already been initiated into holiness through the work of regeneration in order to make this presentation of themselves to God for the purpose of being made entirely holy.

Consecration — Devoting & dedicating a person to worship & service of God. Consecration doesn't make one holy but declares him to be devoted to God or divine service or sacred

"We belong to Him by a twofold claim: First, as the product of His creative power. We are His workmanship in Christ Jesus, both as to original creation by power, and re-creation by grace. Second, we are by His purchase. It is said, *"We are bought with a price;"* that is, a consideration has been given for us. We have been ransomed, not to ourselves, but to God. Original sin put us under a threefold bondage, a triple curse. First, it made us aliens to God, and strangers to the commonwealth of Israel. Second, it made us the slaves of sin and Satan. Third, it made our hearts the seat of corruption and death. Now the purchase-price of Christ's blood has been accepted as a sufficient consideration to justify our complete release."[5]

When we recognize that Satan and sin stole us from God and made us slaves and that Jesus, with His own blood paid our ransom, then consecration, as one man put it, is simply our returning stolen property. *"What! know ye not that your body is the temple of the Holy Ghost which is in you, which ye have of God, and ye are not your own. For ye are bought with a price: therefore glorify God in your body, and in your spirit, which are God's"* (1 Corinthians 6:19-20).

Consecration embraces the whole of man—body, soul and spirit. A complete consecration of one's selfhood is necessary in order to be fully cleansed from sin, and a constant consecration is required in order to maintain a clean heart. As one faithfully walks in the light, the Holy Spirit will make aware of shortcomings that require adjustments to be made in his life. Confessions and occasional acts of repentance may be necessary. Dr. T. M. Anderson used to say, "We must keep the bottom of our *life* up equal to the top of our *light.*" This will be necessary in order for one to stay abreast of the high tide of evil that one will face, and because of the ever enlarging horizon of his spiritual boundaries as he progresses in the faith.

(c.) **Faith** is the conditional cause of man's salvation, both in forgiveness and also in this cleansing work. God purifies the heart by faith (Acts 15:9). The *basis* of our faith is the word of God, and the *object* of our faith is the death of Christ on the cross. All faith rests upon the promises of His word and the provisions of His cross. It is the final word of God that reveals to us the finished work of Calvary.

J. Paul Taylor, speaking of Wesley said, "He never made consecration a distinct step in seeking purity of heart. He constantly proclaimed that the only condition of its reception is faith. What was not explicit in his teaching at this point was clearly implicit, as can be seen by reading the first three pages of his *Plain Account of Christian Perfection*. Consecration was a part of what he called 'a confiding movement.' Every step in the direction of the fullness is a step of faith. It might be put in this form. There is the faith of *conviction*—the fullness is for me. There is the faith of *courage*—I must have it. There is the faith of *committal*—I will have it at all cost. There is the faith of *clasping*—I have it. Every step in the 'confiding movement' is a step of faith in the direction of the promise and the coveted gift. The clasping is the grasp of appropriating faith. The committal or consecration upon which we are dwelling is a most important step in the movement, an act of trust toward the one to whom the soul is committed forever."[6]

In the first work of grace, before faith can operate, repentance is essential. In the second work of grace a complete consecration must precede faith. In other words, consecration is to the second work of grace what repentance is to the first work of grace. Until these pre-requisites are met, man's faith faculty is unable to lay hold of the promises of God.

Unbelief is not always an intellectual problem arising from the lack of evidence, but often times it is a moral problem arising from a lack of willingness. Unbelief is not because one cannot intellectually comprehend salvation in order to exercise faith, but because they refuse to submit either by repentance or consecration, which ever the case may be, in order to believe. Once these conditions are met the hand of faith can reach into the sacred death of the Savior and appropriate the provisions of His cross. It is then that you are able to receive *"the end of your faith, even the salvation of your souls"* (I *Peter 1: 9).* We then are able to lay hold of the promise that *"Christ may dwell in your hearts by faith"* (Ephesians 3:17).

1. **Eldon Fuhrman**, *The Christian Witness*, April 1945

2. **John Wesley**, *Wesley's Works, Sermon XIV The Repentance of Believers*, pp. 168-169

3. **John Wesley**, *Wesley's Works, Sermon XLIII The Scripture Way of Salvation*, p. 45

4. **Roy S. Nicholson**, *True Holiness*, p.16

5. **Asbury Lowrey**, *Possibilities of Grace*, pp. 307-308

6. **J. Paul Taylor,** *Holiness The Finished Foundation,* pp. 47-48

XII.

TERMS IDENTIFYING THE SECOND WORK OF GRACE

This work of grace has been identified by various terms, some scriptural and some non-scriptural. Scriptural terms are entire sanctification (I Thessalonians 5:23), baptism with the Holy Ghost (Matthew 3:11), perfect love (I John 4:18), Christian perfection (Matthew 5:48) and the second rest (Hebrews 4:9). Some of the non-scriptural terms are the second blessing, the deeper life and the victorious life.

This work of God in the heart of man has such far reaching implications that no one term is sufficient to define it. It involves the entire triune Godhead. God the Father planned it; Jesus Christ provided it, and the Holy Spirit accomplishes the work in man's heart. God is the **originating cause** (I Thessalonians 5:23); Jesus is the **provisional cause** (Hebrews 10:10); the Holy Spirit is the **administrative cause** (Romans 15:16); the blood of Christ is the **meritorious cause** (Hebrews 13:12); the word of God is the **instrumental cause** (John 17:17), and faith is the **conditional cause** (Acts 15:9).

Entire Sanctification

Entire sanctification is a second definite work of grace wrought by the baptism with the Holy Spirit in the heart of the believer subsequently to regeneration, received instantly by faith, by which the heart is cleansed from all inward corruption and filled with the perfect love of God. It was provided for us by the blood of Christ, "Wherefore Jesus also, that he might sanctify the people with His own blood, suffered without the gate." Jesus died on the cross that He might restore man to holiness. May we never minimize the sacrifice that He made on the cross by seeking to be entirely sanctified any other way than through the merits of His efficacious blood.

Paul closed his first letter to the Thessalonians with this prayer and benediction: "*And the very God of peace sanctify you wholly; and I pray God your whole spirit and soul and body be preserved blameless unto the coming of our Lord Jesus Christ. Faithful is He that calleth you, who also will do it. Brethren, pray for us. Greet all the brethren with a holy kiss.* **I charge you by the Lord, that this epistle be read unto all the holy brethren.** *The grace of our Lord Jesus Christ be with you. Amen.*" When these brethren read this letter they were going to realize the import of Paul's prayer, the admonition was given to these "**holy brethren**" in order that they would seek and soon be "**sanctified wholly**."

The church at Thessalonica had been formed about six months previous to the writing of this epistle. While they had exhibited exemplary Christian lives, as chapter one reveals, yet in chapter three the apostle was praying night and day for the "perfecting of their faith." In his prayer for their sanctification he was making it quite explicit that God, and not the grave, was their goal; heaven and not the grave-yard is the terminus of our probation. Entire sanctification is not only the supreme requisite and equipment for a life of service in this world but also the one essential qualification for life yet to come.

An initial work of sanctification occurs in regeneration. The second work of grace so transforms the recipients that Paul had to employ the enlarging, qualifying and amplifying word "**wholly**" to differentiate the experience needed to perfect their faith. It is a thorough work of God. It is all of grace, and it is grace for all of man. God sanctifies to all intents and purposes, to the uttermost, through and through. "The God of peace" sanctifies totally.

Bishop Jesse Peck wrote, "To do less for man than to make him holy would be, in effect, to do nothing for him; and to do this is to do all. Holiness is therefore the central sun which pours its glorious light through every part of the system…. remove it, and all is as black as midnight."[1]

Theologian William Burt Pope says, "Sanctification in its beginning, process, and final issue is the full eradication of sin itself which, reigning in the unregenerate, co-exists with the new life of the regenerate, is abolished in the wholly sanctified."[2]

Entire sanctification brings about an integration of the total personality of man and enables him to live in this world, by the grace of God, a life of freedom and normalcy until he is finally resurrected and thereby delivered from the scars and presence of sin itself. When one is sanctified wholly it purifies the heart, preserves one blameless (not faultless) in life and prepares one for the return of our Lord.

Let us state once again that the purpose of the passion of our Lord was to purify (sanctify) His people (Hebrews 13:12). *"Christ also loved the church* [the "called out" ones, the regenerate], *and gave himself for it; that he might sanctify and cleanse it with the washing of water by the word"* (Ephesians 5:25-26). "That inward holiness which the altar ritual of the Hebrews, with their interminable repetitions, was unable to produce, has been rendered possible to every believer through the offering of the adorable God-man once for all. While the atonement sanctified no one, it renders possible the entire sanctification of every offspring of Adam who will trust in Christ for this purchased blessing."[3]

Baptism with the Holy Spirit

The soul wholly sanctified is spoken of as having been baptized *"with the Holy Ghost, and with fire"* (Matthew 3:11). This baptism is distinct from the baptism that John the Baptist performed. His was the baptism *"with water unto repentance"* (Matthew 3:11). John's baptism was ceremonial and was an outward sign of the inward work of God in the regeneration of a sinner. Repentance, evidenced by the fruit of a converted life, was what John required before he ever baptized anyone with water.

When the Pharisees and Sadducees came to be baptized of him in Jordan, John refused to administer this rite to them because they had only a hollow religious formalism to offer him. They had the form without the power and were living on their heritage (Matthew 3:9). It is obvious that those to whom John the Baptist administered water baptism had experienced a work of grace in their hearts that miraculously transformed their lives. One example was an eloquent Jew, mighty in the scriptures, named Apollos. Acts 18:25 tells us that he knew *"only the baptism of John"* until Aquilla and Priscilla *"took him unto them, and expounded unto him the will of God more perfectly."* It was then that Apollos experienced the baptism with the Holy Ghost.

As a physical birth logically precedes a water baptism, so it follows that a spiritual birth precedes the Spirit's baptism. The birth of the Spirit is to be followed by the baptism with the Spirit. John the Baptist taught those he baptized, that, subsequent to his baptism Jesus would come and baptize them with the Holy Ghost. As godly a man as John the Baptist was, he could not perform the baptism with the Holy Ghost. He said, *"He that cometh after me is **mightier** than I, whose shoes I am not **worthy** to bear: He shall baptize you with the Holy Ghost, and with fire"* (Matthew 3:11).

John had neither the <u>might</u> nor the <u>worthiness</u> that only Christ alone possessed to perform this baptism.

Here we have two very different baptisms: John's baptism was ceremonial, but Jesus' baptism is experiential. John's baptism was on the skin, but Jesus' baptism is in the spirit. John's baptism was external, but Jesus' baptism is internal. John used an impersonal agent (water), but Jesus uses a personal agent (Holy Spirit).

John the Baptist was the connecting link between the Old and New Testaments. The Old Testament closes with Malachi's prophecy of a coming Redeemer who would be *"like a refiner's fire, and like fullers' soap,"* and *"sit as a refiner and purifier of silver..."* (Malachi 3:2-3). Four hundred years passed before John the Baptist came as *"the voice of one crying in the wilderness, prepare ye the way of the Lord, make his paths straight"* (Matthew 3:3). He updated the prophecy, declaring, *"He shall baptize you with the Holy Ghost, and with fire."* After His resurrection Jesus met with His disciples and *"commanded them that they should not depart from Jerusalem, but wait for the promise of the Father, which, saith he, ye have heard of me. For John truly baptized with water; but ye shall be baptized with the Holy Ghost not many days hence"* (Acts 1:4). The promise is recorded in the first chapter of Acts, and its fulfillment, occurring on the day of Pentecost, is recorded in the second chapter.

Christian Perfection

No phrase has suffered more abuse and controversy than "Christian perfection." Prejudice and ignorance on this subject, account for much of it. Unbelief and rejection of God's word has prompted some of it. In spite of the abuse and misrepresentation that this term has suffered, perfection is the most frequent term used in the Bible to describe the second work of grace. The word in some form occurs one hundred and thirty-eight times in the Scriptures, and in more than fifty of these instances it refers to human character under the operation of grace. It means that through the cleansing work of the Holy Spirit one can enter into a spiritual completeness or wholeness.

John Wesley admonishes us to avoid setting this perfection too high or too low. We avoid the extremes: "By keeping to the Bible and setting it just as high as the scriptures do. It is nothing higher and nothing lower than this. The pure love of God and man; the loving God with all our heart and soul, and our neighbors as ourselves. It is love governing the heart and life, running through all our tempers, words, and actions."[4] He further submitted the following propositions:

1. There is such a thing as perfection; for it is again and again mentioned in the Scriptures.

2. It is not so early as justification; for justified persons are to "go on unto perfection" (Hebrews 6:1).

3. It is not so late as death; for Paul speaks of living men that were perfect (Philippians 3:15).

4. It is not absolute. Absolute perfection belongs not to men, not to angels, but to God alone.

5. It does not make a man infallible while he remains in the body.

6. Is it sinless? It is not worthwhile to contend for a term. It is 'salvation from sin.

7. It is perfect love (I John 4:18). This is the essence of it; its properties, or inseparable fruits are: rejoicing evermore, praying without ceasing, and in everything giving thanks (I Thessalonians 5:16-18).

8. It is improvable. It is so far from lying in an indivisible point, from being incapable of increase, that one

perfected in love may grow in grace swifter than he did before.

9. It is amissible, capable of being lost; of which we have numerous instances. But we were not thoroughly convinced of this, til five or six years ago.

10. It is constantly both preceded and followed by a gradual work.[5]

In explaining the distinction that needs to be made between involuntary transgressions and voluntary transgressions, Wesley said, "Therefore *sinless perfection* is a phrase I never use, lest I should seem to contradict myself. (4.) I believe, a person filled with the love of God is still liable to these involuntary transgressions. (5.) Such transgressions you may call sins, if you please: I do not, for the reasons above mentioned."[6] However, A. J. Gordon declared, "If the doctrine of sinless perfection is a heresy; the doctrine of contentment with sinful imperfection is a greater heresy. It is not an edifying spectacle to see a Christian worldling throwing stones at a Christian perfectionist."[7]

Joseph H. Smith says, "Man's mind is so constituted as to demand perfection."[8] In our schools where we educate our children we have a grading system. If one receives an "A" on an exam we say that they got a 'perfect' score. We purchase items by weights and standards, and if we go into a market and purchase a pound of cheese we would expect to receive what we paid for, a perfect pound. We would settle for nothing less than perfect fidelity from our mates. In the marital relationship we must be perfectly faithful and loyal to the one to whom we pledged our love. If that love ceases to be true it is apt to bring about a dissolution to the marriage.

God wants our love to be pure and perfect so that we won't engage in spiritual harlotry or become flirtatious with the world. What He commands of His children is "affectional" perfection, for *"Jesus said unto them, thou shalt love the Lord thy God with all thy heart, and with all thy soul, and with all thy mind."* (Matthew 22:37). There is no law in the Bible that exceeds this statute. God requires nothing more; He could demand nothing less. While there is no increase in purity, love is of the same quality as His love and is capable of increase.

An object can be said to be perfect when it fulfills the purpose of its existence. A simple illustration may serve to enlighten us on the concept of perfection. A contractor is hired to build a house and is given the blueprint to follow in its construction. When it is finally completed there may be critics of the structure. One may say that there are too many windows; another may not like the pitch of the roof, and even another may disapprove of the design of the rooms. After listening to all the critics, the contractor has only to go back and submit to them the blueprint and remind them that this was the standard by which he constructed the house and not their varied opinions.

Man was made in God's image and the standard is laid down in the blueprint of His Word. Man has a tendency to measure everything by his own standard, but *"the Lord "seeth not as man seeth; for man looketh on the outward appearance, but the Lord looketh on the heart"* (I Samuel 16:7). We are called to love God and to do His will out of a perfect heart. Jesus commanded, *"Be ye therefore perfect, even as your Father which is in heaven is perfect"* (Matthew 5:48). He makes us adequate to obey the command.

Let us look at some of the scriptural references to perfection:

In Hebrews 11:3 we read, *"Through faith we understand that the worlds were framed by the word of God."* Here the word "framed" translates a Greek word that elsewhere is translated "perfected." This word implies the universe was created to move with perfect precision and coordination. With everything in sync, there would be no disorder. If this creation would ever lose its perfect order and become erratic, this cosmos would become chaotic. The world that God created functions perfectly because the infinite God that created it is also the one who sustains it. *"By Him all things consist."* (Colossians 1:17).

Likewise, He plans for us to live in perfect accord with His will. Christian perfection is that work of God in the soul that enables us to live in harmony with our God.

Jesus *"saw James the son of Zebedee, and John his brother, who also were in the ship **mending** their nets"* (Mark 1:19). The Greek word for perfecting is here rendered "mending." The broken nets had to be repaired in order to catch fish.

There is much about us that is broken because of sin. We are not very useful to Him in our brokenness; we must first be fully mended in order to be fishers of men. We are reminded: *"The God of peace, that brought again from the dead our Lord Jesus, that great Shepherd of the sheep, through the blood of the everlasting covenant **make you perfect in every good work to do His will**"* (Hebrews 13:20-21). Oftentimes, our struggle is not from unwillingness to do His will but from inability to do His will. As Paul said, *"to will is present with me; but how to perform that which is good I find not"* (Romans 7:19-21). God works in us, mending us, so that we have the ability to perform *"every good work."* What He requires of us, He enables and equips us to accomplish.

Another example of this perfection occurs in Paul's injunction, *"Brethren, if a man be overtaken in a fault, ye which are spiritual, **restore** such a one in the spirit of meekness; considering thyself, lest thou also be tempted."*

(Galatians 6:1). Here the Greek word for perfect is translated *"restore."* It carries with it the idea of putting back into place, such as a dislocated arm or leg. To restore means to put back in joint. Sin has thrown us out of joint with God, and He wants to put us perfectly in joint in order that we may do His will.

Christian perfection is the equipment for the task that He wants us to perform. It would be a bit unfair for the Lord to say that we could be fitted for every good work if there is some work that He would call us to do that we were not equipped or qualified to do. But His word assures us that whatever the task He assigns us, He also will furnish the equipment to accomplish the task.

If one chooses to study this topic further there are other Biblical terms to research, such as: the fullness of the Spirit, perfect love, the second rest, the mind of Christ, and heart purity. There have also been other terms that have been used to identify this Christian experience, that, though they are not scripture, per se, they are very scriptural. A few examples are the deeper life, the higher life, the victorious life, and many other phrases.

1. **Bishop Jesse Peck**, *The Central Idea of Christianity*

2. **William Burt Pope**, *A Compendium of Theology*

3. **Daniel Steele**, *The Gospel of the Comforter*, p. 107

4. **John Wesley**, *Plain Account of Christian Perfection*, pp. 44-45

5. **Ibid**, pp.103-104

6. **Ibid**, p. 43

7. **Augustus H. Strong**, *Systematic Theology*, p. 881

8. **Joseph H. Smith**, *Pauline Perfection,* pp. 2-3

XIII.

OTHER THEORIES CONCERNING HOLINESS

All Christians believe that Jesus made provision in the atonement to deliver us from all sin. Controversy arises as to when and where and by what means one is fully free from sin. The various opinions will be presented, and the reader can decide their validity.

First, there is the "**all in one work of grace**" view. Some have taught that one is sanctified wholly at the moment of one's conversion. This view has long been attributed to Count Zinzendorf. "The moment a believer is justified, he is sanctified wholly. Entire sanctification and justification are in the same instant, and neither is increased nor diminished. As soon as one is justified, the Father, the Son, and the Holy Spirit dwell in his heart; and in that moment his heart is as pure as it ever will be"[1]

This teaching is contrary to Scripture and to the teaching of the Early Church. What is more, it is contradicted by the experience of regenerate believers. J. A. Wood, in his book *Perfect Love*, lists some pertinent objections to this view.

1. "If sanctification is complete at justification, then every man that enjoys religion is entirely sanctified.

2. If sanctification is complete at conversion, then every Christian, to be truthful, should *profess* entire sanctification.

3. If all who are converted are entirely sanctified, then all the directions in the Word of God, to seek holiness, sanctification, or perfect love, are given exclusively to sinners.

4. If sanctification is complete at justification, then converts are not to seek for any further cleansing.

5. If sanctification is complete at justification, ministers have no right to urge Christians to "*go on unto perfection*" or to "*cleanse themselves from all filthiness of the flesh and spirit, perfecting holiness in the fear of God.*"

6. If justification and entire sanctification are inseparable, then all who feel the fruits of the flesh are in a state of condemnation.

7. If a state of entire sanctification is consistent with the struggles of *pride, unbelief, impatience, jealously*, and *anger* (the common experience of newly justified believers), must we not infer that these must go with us to heaven? as it must be admitted that entire sanctification fits the soul for heaven.

8. If sanctification is complete at justification, then every man who is not entirely sanctified is a child of the devil.

9. If entire sanctification is complete at justification, it is so in opposition to the experience of the whole church of God; and, with slight exceptions, the whole Christian world has been seriously mistaken during two thousand years.

10. If all that are regenerate are wholly sanctified, then whoever is convicted for full salvation, and groaning after it, is at once to infer that he was never converted, or that he is now backslidden. Thus would this heresy, if received, perplex and harass with per-

petual difficulties and discouragements the very members of the church who are most deeply concerned to possess the mind of Christ.

A system involving such difficulties cannot be received as the Truth of God, and should be regarded as anti-scriptural and avoided as dangerous heresy."[2]

Secondly, there is the **"growing into sanctification"** view. It is necessary that we say right up front that growth in grace is essential to life. In order for spiritual life to be maintained there must be a continual development of the Christian character. Growth is a sign of life. However there must be a distinction between growing *in* grace and growing *into* grace. One may swim in the pool, but one does not swim into the pool. He must enter into the water before he can swim in it. There is growth previous to entire sanctification, in fact it is preliminary preparation for it, and the experience itself is condition for more rapid and greater growth that shall follow.

However, the teaching that one grows *into* entire sanctification as a gradual experience does not square with God's Word. If we subscribe to such teaching, then time becomes a factor, to some a liability and to others an asset, determined by how long or short one lives. Those who enjoy a long life span have an advantage over those who have a short life span. It also teaches an approximation toward a goal that discourages one's faith in the merits of the blood that can cleanse from sin even now.

Those who teach this view strongly insist that our regeneration is not by works but by grace. This we all believe and hold to as being scriptural. *"For by grace are ye saved through faith; and that not of your selves: it is the gift of God"* (Ephesians 2:8). But when it comes to entire sanctification they teach that it is all of works and growth. It was the very thing that the Apostle Paul was critical of, concerning those in Galatia who had begun in the Spirit by the hearing of faith and were then trying to be made perfect (sanctified) by the flesh. He said, *"O foolish Galatians, who hath bewitched you, that you should not obey the truth"* (Galatians 3:1). He taught in the previous chapter that righteousness doesn't come by keeping the law; if it did then Christ died in vain. He warned them about "frustrating" (nullifying) the grace of God. When we depend on anything other than the blood of Christ for our cleansing from sin then we nullify and make void His grace.

Those who believe that entire sanctification is received by growth need to recognize that entire sanctification is a condition of growth. As quaint as it may sound, one does not expect that the growth of a garden will eradicate the weeds. It has been my experience that the weeds, if not plucked up by their roots, will stunt the growth of the garden. So if sin is allowed to remain in the heart, and we depend on growth, rather than the blood of Christ, to free us from sin, it will choke the life of God out of our souls.

I recall evangelist Dr. John Church telling about conversing with an elderly man who believed that he could be sanctified wholly by growth in grace. Dr. Church asked him how long he had been a Christian, and the gentleman said that he had been a Christian over fifty years. Dr. Church asked if he had grown into it yet, to which the man answered, "Not yet but I'm pressing toward it." Dr. Church then admonished, "You had better get in quickly because you don't have many years left." Church went on to suggest to the gentleman, "After all these years of trying to grow into the experience and not having yet received it, why not give faith a try and trust God to do it now?" He did and God sanctified him wholly by faith, and he lived the rest of his days growing in grace until God took him home.

Samuel Chadwick made these distinctions: "Holiness does not come by growth, neither is it identified by growth. Growth is a process of life; holiness is the gift of abundant life. Growth is the result of health; holiness is health. Holiness implies a crisis, a new experience, a transformed life. It is not an achievement nor an attainment, but a gift of grace in the Holy Ghost"[3]

Thirdly, there is what we will call the "**Holy-in-Christ**" view. Those who teach this view, often misconstrue the phrase, "holy in Christ" and create a dangerous error. They do not teach real deliverance from sin. The holiness that they teach is ours by "standing." They illustrate it by suggesting that Christ's covering of our sin is like a blanket of snow that covers the barnyard, and when God looks upon us He doesn't see the ugliness of our sin, but He sees only Christ's righteousness, although we are still very sinful He accounts us as being righteous because Christ is righteous. Someone asked the question with reference to the barnyard blanketed with snow, "What happens when it thaws?"

It is possible to expound the words, "holy in Christ," in such a way that all is objective and potential, and little or nothing actual and experiential. We readily acknowledge the holiness in Christ, but Paul's concern was about actually getting His holiness into us. It is not merely an imputed righteousness but an imparted righteousness; we are made *"partakers of His holiness"* (Hebrews 12:10). It is not our working and striving to be holy but rather His holiness imparted to us until ours is the out-living of His indwelling. The Holy Spirit, as the executive agent of the God-head, came to make *actual* all that Jesus provided and made *potential* in His death and resurrection. The Holy Spirit is the divinely appointed agent to make real *in* us what Christ provided *for* us.

While we believe Christ is the source and standard of all holiness, that fact does not preclude man's responsibility. God's Word does teach that holiness is imputed where light and obligation are as yet unknown. For example, a child before he reaches the age of accountability enjoys imputed righteousness. This is true of anyone who is ignorant of the full privileges of God's grace. The blood of Christ unconditionally atones for their sins of ignorance. However, the time will come when one receives light, and then he must, by faith, become a partaker of Christ's holiness.

The Old Testament presents salvation by representation. The High Priest alone could enter into the holy of holies to represent the people. When Jesus died on the cross, the veil that separated the holy place from the holy of holies was rent from top to bottom, and we now have access into the holiest by the blood of Christ. The Christian no longer needs to be represented by an earthly high priest because we have a heavenly Priest to Whom we can bring our petitions. Instead of salvation by mere representation we now have a salvation by participation. We now can enter into the holiest and become partakers of His holiness. It is a holiness that is not reckoned ours merely by proxy but actually received by faith.

Fourthly, there is the view that one receives this deliverance from sin at the time of death. This is the "**dying grace**" view. Some conclude that the fleshly body is the seat of sin and teach, as the Gnostics taught, that all matter is evil.

If one subscribes to this view then he would have to believe that the larger one is in the body the greater sinner he would be. He would have to believe that God who created the body would be the originator of sin. They would also have to believe that the incarnate Christ, while in the flesh on earth, would have been sinful. They also would be teaching that death, not the blood of Christ, would be our deliverer even though God's Word teaches us that death is the last enemy to be destroyed.

Fifthly, there is the **Catholic view** that deliverance from sin comes after death through the sufferings of purgatory. Trusting in prayer vigils and candle lightings by the living, they then would put their faith in the fires of purgatory in hope of deliverance by and by. This view presumes that one, by involuntary suffering after death, can atone for their voluntary sin prior to death. If this is true, then Jesus' death was needless and would have been the highest act of injustice that could have ever been committed by a Holy God.

The fact of the matter is, there have never been any actual witnesses who have come forth to testify that they have experienced cleansing from all sin by any of these theories.

a. There is no one who could testify to being entirely sanctified at the time of conversion. When they say they "got it all at once," they mean that they got all they got at once, but that is not all there was to get.

b. No one can document that at a moment in time, through growth, they grew into entire sanctification. No one has ever testified that at a certain hour or moment they entered into the experience of entire sanctification by growth.

c. The "imputed" view does not believe in being fully delivered in this life.

d. There are no witnesses to those who claim to get it in the hour and article of death. If they got it by "dying grace" it was only because they waited until then to believe for it. They could have believed and received it long before death if they only would have.

e. No one has ever come back from the fires of purgatory to testify to having been purged from sin after death.

While there has never been anyone who has witnessed to the work of entire sanctification through any of the above theories, there have been multiplied thousands who have testified, and even now can testify, that following an act of total consecration they received the baptism with the Holy Spirit by faith and were made pure in heart.

"Holiness (*entire sanctification, Christian perfection*), is relative to our creaturely experience and earthly limitations; derived from God's grace in Christ, not based on any merit of our own; progressive, or capable of indefinite improvement; alienable, or forfeitable; not guaranteed to perpetuity, but conditional on faith, our striving against sin, and steadfast abiding in the love of God..."[4] (Italics are mine)

Consider the summary by evangelist, Russell V. DeLong:

"Holiness is theologically sound; theoretically reasonable; philosophically the highest good; psychologically desirable; ethically imperative; sociologically necessary; Biblically commanded; practically satisfying; and experientially, gloriously possible."

Therefore, let us study it carefully, seek it diligently, secure it promptly, and scatter it globally."[5]

1. **John Wesley**, *Wesley's Works, Sermon XIII, (Argument against Zinzendorf)* pp. 149- 150.

2. **J. A. Wood**, *Perfect Love*, pp. 27-28

3. **Samuel Chadwick**, *The Way to Pentecost*

4. **Roy S. Nicholson**, (A quote in his book *True Holiness*, p.33)

5. **Roy S. Nicholson,** *True Holiness*, p. 33

XIV.

NECESSARY DISTINCTIONS

God created man in His own image. He looked upon His creation, including Adam and Eve, and pronounced it "very good." His approval was placed upon humanity.

Christian theology has distinguished between the natural image and the moral image of God in man. In the fall, the moral image of God was forfeited, and this is restored through Christ, "in righteousness and true holiness." The natural image, while greatly impaired and scarred, was not lost in the fall.

God does not destroy in redemption what He made in creation. Sin, as an intruder, has marred God's creation. God does not intend to dehumanize man, but He has made provisions to rid us of the intruder, sin. It is not sinful to be human; a human is sinful as the result of carnality. God does not dehumanize man, but He seeks to de-carnalize (to coin a word) the human. It is unbiblical to equate being human with being sinful; otherwise, God would have been the creator of sin. God is not at odds with our humanity but rather with carnality.

A question often asked is how anyone could ever sin again once sin has been cleansed. The answer is, in the same way that the first pair sinned in the Garden of Eden. A wrong use was made of the freedom of choice with which God endowed all mankind. If sin could enter into the first pair in the Garden, despite the perfection that they enjoyed in body and mind, may it not re-enter a cleansed human personality that now suffers the scars of sin resulting from fallibilities of the mind and infirmities of the body? Full redemption does not render us unable to sin, but it makes us able not to sin. In this life of probation, we are able to sin if we choose to, but grace enables us not to sin regardless of the pressure put upon us by the enemy.

Resisting sin, John Wesley taught, requires a moment by moment dependence on Christ as Prophet, Priest and King. "The holiest of men still need Christ, as their Prophet, as the light of the world. For He does not give them light, but from moment to moment; the instant He withdraws, all is darkness. They still need Christ as their King; for God does not give them a stock in holiness. But unless they receive a supply every moment, nothing but unholiness would remain. They still need Christ as their Priest, to make atonement for their holy things. Even perfect holiness is acceptable to God only through Jesus Christ."[1]

Failure to recognize that humanity is not inherently sinful has caused a great deal of misunderstanding and false teaching about the doctrine of holiness. God pronounced His entire creation, including human beings, *"very good"* (Genesis 1:31). Because of the fall of man, the malady of sin has infected humanity, and this deadly disease, carnality, the malady of the soul, has greatly impaired its functioning. It has brought about scars and limitations that all persons will suffer as long as they are in this present world. Entire Sanctification is that work of God's grace that cleanses the heart from carnality, but man must be faithful to walk in obedience to the light and rely on the cleansing blood, ministered by God's grace, as long as he is in this present world.

Man was made in the image and likeness of God, and that likeness included a natural image as well as a moral image. The natural image consisted of man's intellect, which gave to him the power of reason; he also was created an emotional creature, and he has a volitional capacity that gives him the power of will and choice. The moral image consisted of holiness and righteousness. The moral image was lost in the fall while the natural image, while marred was not destroyed, and the damage must be remedied through grace.

Sin and Infirmity

The difference between humanity and carnality is that humanity can be disciplined to obey the law of God, but the Apostle Paul tells us: *"The carnal mind is enmity against God: for it is not subject* (cannot be made to submit) *to the law of God, neither indeed can be"* (Romans 8:7). While sin is grounded in the moral nature, infirmities are grounded in human nature. As J. A. Woods observed: "Many who reject the Doctrine of Christian Perfection confound infirmities and sins. Infirmities may entail regret and humiliation. Sin always produces guilt"[2]

Daniel Steele insisted on this same distinction. "Infirmities are failures to keep the law of perfect obedience given to Adam and Eve. This law no man on earth can keep, since sin has impaired the powers of universal humanity. Sins are offences against the law of Christ.... Infirmities are an involuntary outflow from our imperfect moral organization. Sin is always voluntary.... Infirmities in well-instructed souls do not interrupt communion with God. Sin cuts the telegraphic communication with heaven.... Infirmities are without remedy so long as we are in this body. Sins, by the keeping power of Christ, are avoidable through every hour of our regenerate life. Both of these truths are in Jude's ascription, *'Now unto Him that is able to keep you from falling* [into sin] *and present you faultless* [without infirmity, not here, but] *in the presence of His glory with exceeding joy.'* Jude understood the distinction between faults, or infirmities, and sins. In this scheme of Christian perfection, faults are to disappear in the life to come, but we are to be saved from sins now.... A thousand infirmities are consistent with perfect love, but not one sin"[3]

When Jesus took upon himself the form of our humanity, while He did not divest himself of His deity, He set aside the prerogatives of His deity for a while in order to subject himself to the limitations, humiliations and dependency of a man. He understands our plight and has become our sympathetic High Priest. As a result, *"We have not an high priest which cannot be touched with the feelings of our infirmities; but was in all points tempted like as we are, yet without sin"* (Hebrews 4:15). He intercedes on our behalf and provides grace sufficient for the hour. *"My grace is sufficient for thee: for my strength is made perfect in weakness. Most gladly therefore will I rather glory in my infirmities, (not sin), that the power of Christ may rest upon me"* (II Corinthians 12:9). Paul is very careful to distinguish sin from infirmities. In Romans 6:1-2, Paul asks a rhetorical question: *"Shall we continue in sin, that grace may abound?"* He immediately provides the answer to his question, *"God forbid. How shall we, that are dead to sin, live any longer therein?"* (Romans 6:1-2). Paul certainly did not glory in sin but, according to II Corinthians 12:9, he gloried in his infirmities in order that the power of Christ might rest upon him.

Lacks and limitations, ignorance and infirmities, do not condemn us. These may produce humiliation, but they do not produce condemnation. Only sin produces condemnation. However even our infirmities and mistakes require the benefits of the atonement. This is why Wesley said: "The best of men still need Christ in His priestly office to atone for their omissions, their shortcomings (as some now improperly speak), their mistakes in judgment and practice, and their defects of various kinds. For these are all deviations from the perfect law, and consequently need an atonement. Yet that they are not properly sins we apprehend may appear from the words of St. Paul: *'He that loveth another hath fulfilled the law... for love is the fulfilling of the law'"* (Romans 13:8-10).

Perfect Love and Conduct

It has already been stated that man's essential nature is limited, restricted and finite, and as such we are creatures of errors and mistakes. While man can have a pure heart he does not have an infallible mind. Therein lies the difference between motive and method. Motive is *heart planning,* but method is *head planning.* Both method and motive must be correct in order for one to come out with a proper consequence. If one's motive is pure but his performance or method is flawed, wrong consequences will result. God does not condemn us for a wrong method, but He will correct and chasten us through love so that we will be more effective witnesses for Him. While God looks on the heart, man sees our actions and hears our words and will judge us, accordingly. The world doesn't see Christ crowned within us. They do see the Christian conduct that exudes from us. Because we are called to be His witnesses and we are representatives of Christ, we do not want to say or do anything that will bring reproach upon Him. When the God of Peace sanctifies the believers wholly, they are <u>preserved blameless</u> and one day he will be <u>presented faultless</u> before the Father. Until the day when we will be presented faultless, it is incumbent upon the 'sanctified wholly' to work to close the gap between blameless and faultless living as near as possible, knowing in this life he never will close it completely.

The perfection that God calls the believer to is a relative perfection, and this perfection does not exempt us from error and mistakes. It is human to err. In preaching or

105

teaching holiness, unless we take into account the human element, we will put the standard where it cannot be reached. Perfect love will not produce a perfect body, a perfect mind, nor will it produce a perfect conduct. Infallibility is not the fruit of holiness.

I recall an evangelist telling a story about his two sons. The eldest son had obediently carried out a chore that his father had asked him to do. The father told him how proud he was of such an obedient son. Standing off to the side was his younger son who wanted his father to tell him how proud he was of him also. It was a very warm day, and the father was in his office working on a sermon when his younger son brought him a glass of water to drink. The little boy carried the glass of water with muddy fingers bent over the brim of the glass and with mud clouding the water. He looked up into his father eyes and asked, "Are you proud of me too, father?" The father took the boy up in his arms and told him how proud he was and how much he loved him. The little boy's action was a bit flawed, but it did not diminish his father's love for him. In fact, because it was such an act of love, it probably deepened his love for his young son.

God does not condemn us because of our faults and failures or because of the lack and limitations of humanity, even though they mar performance, He looks to the motives of our hearts. He doesn't demand perfect performance but rather perfect love. When He controls our heart and life our actions are motivated by love. Our life becomes a labor of love rendered for our Savior and for the souls of men.

Christian Security and Unconditional Security

No degree of grace can put us where we cannot fall. "There is no state of grace so high that once you reach it you will soon discover that there has been one who has preceded you there and has fallen from that holy place into sin" (Joseph H. Smith).

While there is no state of grace that will put us where we *cannot* fall, there is a state of grace that can put us where we *need* not fall. Entire sanctification does not destroy our capacity to sin; but it does destroy our bent to sinning and proclivity to sin. It is imperative that we keep our minds disciplined and pure, the Psalmist said, *"I will set no wicked thing before mine eyes"* (Psalms 101:3). As the angels and our first parents fell, so we can fall by the natural laws of the mind. They thought themselves away from God. The serpent in the garden made his appeal to Eve's rationale, which in turn, created an intense desire for that which was forbidden which resulted in the act of disobedience. Obedience to an Infinite God's word and will was on trial in the Garden. The test was not to satisfy the rationale of man's finite mind. Nothing God instructs and demands are unreasonable, but many things do transcend man's reason. Evil thinking always precedes evil practice.

That is why the Apostle Paul admonishes: *"Finally, brethren, whatsoever things are true, whatsoever things are honest,, whatsoever things are just, whatsoever things are pure, whatsoever things are lovely, whatsoever things are of good report; if there be any virtue, and if there be any praise,* **think on these things***"* (Philippians 4:8).

There are some who teach that once a Christian, one will always be a Christian; once saved, always saved. Such teaching advocates that the will of man is abolished once he becomes a child of God. If that were true every admonition, caution, warning, and condition given to the Christian in God's Word has no meaning or merit. Such a passage as 2 Peter 2:5-10 would be nonsense: *"Giving all diligence, add to your faith virtue; and to virtue knowledge; and to knowledge, temperance; and to temperance, patience; and to* *patience, godliness; and to godliness, brotherly kindness; and to brotherly kindness, charity. For if these be in you, and abound, they make you that ye shall neither be barren nor unfruitful in the knowledge of our Lord Jesus Christ. But he that lacketh these things is blind, and cannot see afar off, and hath forgotten that he was purged from his old sins. Wherefore the rather, brethren, give diligence to make your calling and election sure: <u>for if ye do these things, ye shall never fall</u>.*" It must, therefore be possible to fall!

As one can "*think*" himself away from God, even so he must exercise his mind in order to come back to God. Faith begins in the head: "*So then faith cometh by hearing, and hearing by the word of God*" (Romans 10:17). The head must be convinced if the heart is to be convicted and converted. However, with that being said, the Apostle Paul teaches that it is more than an intellectual process for in Romans 10:10 we read, "*For with the <u>heart</u> man believeth unto righteousness; and with the <u>mouth</u> confession is made unto salvation.*"

✓ Retaining Holiness in the Heart and Life

Many things are necessary for the retention of holiness of heart and life. The Christian life is not like a self-winding watch. Confession, vigilance, prayer, study and obedience are necessary to continued growth in the Christian faith.

<u>Public testimonials and confessions</u> of His work in our lives are important, though some say that it is not necessary to profess the experience, only to express it in the life. We readily agree that one should live out what he professes, but we strongly disagree that testimony to holiness is needless. John Fletcher lost the experience of sanctification several times because he refused to openly and verbally testify to it. That one should testify to it is affirmed by God's word:

"With the mouth confession is made unto salvation" (Romans 10:10).

John Fletcher confessed that he had lost the experience of heart purity four or five times by refusing to confess it, he says: "I declare unto you, in the presence of God, the *Holy Trinity*, I am 'now dead indeed unto sin.' I do not say 'I am crucified with Christ,' because some of our well-meaning brethren say by this can only be meant a gradual dying; but I profess unto you, I am dead unto sin and alive unto God! And remember, all this is 'through Jesus Christ our Lord.' He is my *Prophet, Priest,* and *King*; my indwelling holiness; my *all in all*."[4]

I recall a minister pressing home the importance of a believer verbally testifying to the sanctifying work of God in the heart. He told of a man who had a disease that would prove fatal if no cure was found. He went to a doctor who diagnosed his disease and recommended a surgical procedure that would likely produce a cure and insure long life. The sick man submitted to the doctor's care and the surgeon's hand and was made physically whole. The preacher then asked the question, "What if this healed man became aware of someone suffering with the same disease from which he had been delivered? Should he tell him about the doctor or just live a healthy life before him?" The answer is obvious. He should testify to the healing and commend the doctor. When Jesus has sanctified us we should share it with those who need cleansing from all sin. The notion that we should merely live holy before them without talking to them about the one who made us spiritually whole is ludicrous. We must herald it to the world as the hymn writer wrote:

"Holiness forever more!

Holiness forever more!

We will sing it, shout it,

Preach it, and live it,

Holiness forevermore!"

(Haldor Lillenas)

When Wesley was asked if it would not be better to be silent, and not to speak of holiness, He answered: "By silence, he might avoid many crosses, which will naturally and necessarily ensue, if he simply declare, even among believers, what God has wrought in his soul. If, therefore, such a one were to confer with flesh and blood, he would be entirely silent. But this could not be done with a clear conscience: for undoubtedly he ought to speak. Men do not light a candle to put under a bushel; much less does the all wise God. He does not raise such a monument of his power and love, to hide it from all mankind. Rather, he intends it as a general blessing to those who are simple of heart. He designs thereby, not barely the happiness of that individual person, but the animating and encouraging others to follow after the same blessing. His will is, 'that many shall see it' and rejoice, 'and put their trust in the Lord.' Nor does anything under heaven more quicken the desires of those who are justified, than to converse with those whom they believe to have experienced a still higher salvation. This places that salvation full in their view, and increases their hunger and thirst after it; an advantage which must have been entirely lost, had the person so saved buried himself in silence."[5]

✓ Vigilance is important in retaining our relationship with Christ. *"See then that ye walk circumspectly, not as fools, but as wise, redeeming the time, because the days are evil"* (Ephesians 5:15-16). We must *"Put on the whole armor of God, that ye may be able to stand against the wiles of the devil. For we wrestle not against flesh and blood, but against*

110

principalities, against powers, against the rulers of the darkness of this world, against spiritual wickedness in high places" (Ephesians 6:11-12). We must be faithful students of the word of God and have our loins girt about with truth.

In the study of the word of God we receive light for our journey. Richard Watson says, "The Word of God is the food of faith." John tells us in his first epistle that there are conditions that must be met in order to retain fellowship with Christ and enjoy the continual cleansing of sin through the merits of His blood. Five times in I John 1:6-10 the little word "if" occurs. It is the conditional hinge upon which swing the promises of God. If we obey His word this hinge swings us into light, life and fellowship with Christ. If we disobey it swings us into darkness and death with the damned.

Prayer is essential to the Christian life. We must pray *"always with all prayer and supplication in the Spirit, and watching thereunto with all perseverance and supplication for all saints"* (Ephesians 6:18). Our prayer should consist of communion, petition and intercession. Prayer reaches first of all upward in adoration to God. It then moves inward to meet our personal needs. Finally it stretches outward to the needs of others. The provisions and promises of God, revealed in His word, are the premises of our prayers.

Faith is another essential element in the retention of holiness. Our faith rests on the finished work of Christ and the final word of God. Faith is not blind credulity when one stands on His word; it is *"the substance of things hoped for, the evidence of things not seen."* (Hebrews 11:1). Faith is *substance* and *evidence*. Timothy Dwight said, "The faith of the Gospel is the emotion of the mind which is called trust or confidence, exercised toward the moral character of God, and particularly of the Savior" (Works, Volume II, p. 326). We should remember that some things in the spiritual realm do not lend themselves to the definitions of the finite mind. Through faith we are able to appropriate some things in the heart that we are unable to comprehend in the head.

For example, Nicodemus did not understand how one could be born again. He even asks, *"How can a man be born when he is old? can he enter the second time into his mother's womb, and be born?"* Jesus said, *"The wind bloweth where it listeth, and thou hearest the sound thereof, but canst not tell whence it cometh, and whither it goeth: so is every one that is born of the Spirit"* (John 3:4, 8). Like the wind, we can feel it, hear it, see the effects of it, and know something is transpiring, but we cannot fully grasp it with our finite mind. That is why the writer of Hebrews reminds us: *"Without faith it is impossible to please Him: for he that cometh to God must believe that He is, and that He is a rewarder of them that diligently seek Him"* (Hebrews 11:6).

A continual obedience to His Word is a requirement for discipleship. *"If ye continue in my word, then are ye my disciples indeed; and ye shall know the truth, and the truth shall make you free"* (John 8:31, 32). The key word is "continue," because, once again we are taught that a man may be holy and not yet established in holiness. Truth becomes the instrument of our freedom, as Jesus prayed in John 17:17, *"Sanctify them through thy truth: thy word is truth."* When one experiences the purifying of the heart, it becomes a stepping-stone to growth and development of Christian character. Most of our growth is beyond heart-purity. With all hindrances to growth removed, one should grow more rapidly than before.

Temptation and Sin

Many people have falsely reasoned that if one is completely delivered from sin then temptation could no longer be possible. Those who arrive at such a conclusion make sin the ground or source of temptation. They further state that if one is tempted to sin then sin must be resident in the heart. They fail to take into account that Adam and Eve were pure in their hearts before they ever yielded to temptation and sinned. Also, the sinless Son of God was led in the wilderness to be tempted of the devil. Sin was certainly not the source of His temptation.

The true source or ground for temptation is not sin but man's volitional character. Man was given freedom to make choices, and the devil makes his appeal to man's will, tempting him to yield and commit sin. *"But every man is tempted, when he is drawn away of his own lust* [human desire], a*nd enticed. Then when lust hath conceived, it bringeth forth sin; and sin, when it is finished, bringeth forth death"* (James 1:14-15). It should be noticed that the word "lust" is simply the God-given, human desires, appetites, and passions. Sin occurs when one yields to temptation and the human passions and desires are expressed without regards to God's will, or expressed outside the bounds of God's will.

For example, food is necessary to sustain the body, but when one over indulges, eating becomes the sin of gluttony. God has made man to procreate the human race, and therefore sex is a legitimate human drive, but if it is expressed outside the bounds of His law of love, it is a perversion and becomes sin.

The Christian must always yield to the mastery of the Holy Spirit. He must keep his mind and affections on things above. The serpent first got the mind of Eve, and it resulted in the sin of disobedience. It has been said that what gets our mind will ultimately get us. If temptation overcomes the mind it will seek consent of the emotions and sensibilities, and finally the will of man will be engaged, and the sinful act will be born.

In the Garden (Genesis 3) the serpent made his first approach to the mind (reason) of Eve. *"Yea, hath God said, ye shall not eat of every tree of the garden?"* Here he planted suspicion in her mind about God. He suggested that perhaps God was not being true and fair. It wasn't long until he appealed to her sensibilities when he suggested to her that *"it was a tree to be desired to make one wise."* She was then just a step away from engaging her will and committing the act of disobedience, for *"She took of the fruit thereof, and did eat, and gave also unto her husband with her; and he did eat."* The rest is history as sin and death passed upon the whole human race. When temptation is yielded to, *"lust conceives and brings forth sin and when it is finished it brings forth death."* The fact is that sin is very progressive. If temptation is yielded to and sin is conceived, it will take one farther than he thought he would ever go, and he will do what he thought he would never do. The nature of sin is such that it destroys one's capacity to know its progress. Therefore we must, by God's help, guard our heart.

Temptations will come from many directions. *"Wherefore let him that thinketh he standeth take heed lest he fall. There hath no temptation taken you but such as is common to man: but God is faithful, who will not suffer you to be tempted above that ye are able; but will with the temptation also make a way to escape, that ye may be able to bear it"* (I Corinthians 10:11-12).

Purity and Maturity

As I have already stated, the work of entire sanctification is primarily that of subtraction not addition. It is the removal of that which is alien to man from creation. It is the removal of the lodger—sin—and the enthronement of our Lord and Savior. It takes the dross out of the gold and wax out of the honey. It is the burning up of the chaff, and the gathering and preserving of the wheat. Entire sanctification does not give us anything different in kind than what we received in regeneration. We receive all we ever get in kind when we are converted. The difference is one of degree but not one of kind. Every element in a towering oak is present in a little sapling. When converted one receives love; when sanctified wholly that love is made perfect. When converted one receives joy; when sanctified wholly he experiences the fullness of joy.

Unlike maturity, the pure heart experiences no increase. There is no such thing as being pure and then more pure. When one is pure in heart, *the eye is single and the whole body is full of light.* The graces exist in an unmixed state. Love exists without any germs of hatred, faith without any unbelief, humility without pride, meekness without anger. Purity of heart is the removal of whatever God could not admit to His immediate presence, and fellowship with Himself; in other words, the abolition of sin itself"[6]

Purity of heart has reference to kind or quality, but maturity has respect to degree or quantity. Therefore, holiness is both a crisis and a process, and as such, it is both instantaneous and gradual. The process should be as glorious as the crisis. In fact, regained health through convalescence is more desirable than the relief of crisis by surgery. Purity of heart is accomplished by the work of the Spirit of God; maturity is the result of years of obedient living.

To illustrate the difference between the crisis and process of holiness let us examine the experience and life of a bride and bridegroom. There are first the days of courtship between the two parties that lead up to an engagement. They have, by entering into this engagement, pledged their loyalty and faithfulness to one another while preparing for the wedding day. During these days they share their love for each other by giving gifts, sending cards, enjoying intermittent times together. The wedding day arrives, and they stand before God and witnesses, and they pronounce their vows of the love covenant to one another. This lays the foundation for the marriage that will follow for years to come. The years of the marriage will require many adjustments and corrections, but these can be made without breaking their vows.

Let us consider the engagement as the crisis of the new birth. Following that experience there will come a time when one will be called upon to make a total abandonment of himself to His Savior. This is a very decisive act, all-embracing for present and future, and should never need to be done again. We liken this to the wedding vows that are necessary to finalize the wedding. Marriage is not to be done conditionally, or as an experiment, or contingent on how we feel the next day, it should be an irrevocable decision. So it is with the Christian life. As it was in the wedding, so must it be in this holy covenant the believer makes with God. Repentance and faith that results in the new birth, is followed by the believer's consecration and faith which results in the work of entire sanctification. These two experiences are done at two separate and distinct points in time, which initiates (lays the foundation) for the development of the Christ-like life that continues thereafter. But the working out of the mature Christian character is a life long endeavor that will require many adjustments, like the working out of the marriage following the wedding.

"Purity is the entrance into Canaan; maturity is the possession of the land.

Purity is received, but maturity is acquired. Purity is the work of a moment, while maturity is the harvest of years. Purity is always received by faith, but maturity is often reached through pain. Purity has to do with quality, while maturity has to do with quantity. Purity fits the soul for heaven, but maturity acquires material for reward."[7]

"The Apostle John in his first epistle gave us a threefold distinction of Christian believers: <u>little children</u>, <u>young men</u>, and <u>fathers</u>. All of these had received the Holy Ghost, but only the fathers were perfected in love."[8]

"Both Wesley and Fletcher and their contemporaries did not stress the 'state of holiness' lest they seem to encourage settling down immediately following the crisis experience. (They did not want to make holiness static or stagnant, *my words!*). But they emphasized what Thomas Cook has described as maintaining the 'condition of purity.' That is 'a moment by moment salvation consequent upon a moment by moment obedience and trust. *'The blood of Jesus Christ cleanses us from all sin'* all the time by cleansing us even now."[9] (Thomas Cook's statement is found in his *New Testament Holiness*, p. 43 in chapter entitled, "The Present Tense of Cleansing.")

Perfect in love is not spiritual finality but spiritual fitness. Being now made perfect in love one is enabled to develop and grow more rapidly in the grace of God. He is made ready for the race. Running the race, or 'perfecting holiness,' should characterize the sanctified believer, after the work of cleansing has been made complete; that is, in the development and maturity of all the Christian graces and, the development of the fruit of the Spirit."[10]

1. **John Wesley**, *Plain Account of Christian Perfection*, p. 71

2. **J. A. Wood**, *Perfect Love*, p. 66

3. **Daniel Steele**, *Milestone Papers*, pp. 33-35

4. **Hester Ann Rogers**, (Writing about Fletcher, in *Scriptural Way of Holiness*, W. McDonald) p. 247

5. **John Wesley**, *Plain Account of Christian Perfection*, pp. 45-46

6. **Thomas Cook**, *New Testament Holiness*, pp. 33-34

7. **Harry Jessop**, *Foundations of Doctrine*, p. 134

8. **Roy S. Nicholson**, *True Holiness*, p. 68

9. **Ibid**, pp. 68-69

10. **Ibid**, p. 69

XV.

VISUALS THAT ILLUSTRATE THE SECOND WORK OF GRACE

I remember several years ago reading a sermon by Leslie R. Marston, a former Bishop of the Free Methodist Church. I thought that the diagrams that he provided in his sermon were very good as they clarify the two works of grace very instructively as well as visually. I wanted to submit them in this book with the hope that it will aid someone in their pursuit and understanding of the holiness message. I will present each diagram as Dr. Marston presented them in the book that contained his message.

1. The following is a diagram that represents the *human nature under the dominion of sin.* For the sake of clarity we will call this the *'natural man.'* *"The natural man receiveth not the things of the Spirit of God: for they are foolishness unto him: neither can he know them, because they are spiritually discerned."* (I Corinthians 2:14).

This man is the man that Paul says is, *"dead in trespasses and sins;...he walks according to the course of this world, according to the prince of the power of the air, the spirit that now worketh in the children of disobedience...he is by nature the children of wrath....having no hope, and without God in the world."* (Ephesians 2:1, 2, 3 and 12).

Marston says, "All traits here appear in black to indicate the dominion of sin, and the lines issuing from them lead to overt sin. There will be those to protest that man is never a sinner in all of his traits; that at some point in every man's life, however vile, goodness is expressed. To this I readily assent, but the diagram represents unregenerate human nature totally depraved in the sense that there is in man of himself by nature and apart from grace nothing by which he achieves holiness or merits salvation."

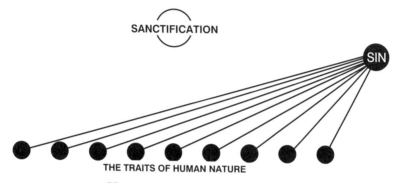

Chart 1. The Dominion of Sin
"For when we were servants of sin, ye were free from righteousness."—Romans 6:20

✓   2. The next diagram represents *human nature under the disputed dominion of grace.* We will call this man the *"yet carnal"* man. He has received the regenerating grace of God. He is no longer *"dead in his sins,"* but he is manifesting characteristics in his disposition that reveals he is lacking something in his faith. Paul says that there is *envying, and strife, and divisions, are ye not carnal, and walk as men?"* He is better than he used to be but not as good as he ought to be; because he has not been sanctified entirely he can feed only on the milk diet and is unable to digest the meat of God's word. He is in danger of moving from a child-like spirit to a childish spirit. (I Corinthians 3:1-3).

Marston said, "The traits of human nature here appear in black and white to designate the *double mind*—the mind of righteousness implanted by grace designated by the white portion, the mind of sin to which humanity is heir by fallen nature designated by the black portion. The lines leading from these traits are accordingly bent or kinked toward sin, but finally issues in righteousness, for the unsanctified Christian does not commit overt sin even though the principle of sin rankles within.

How can man with the mind to sin avoid the act of sin? There are at least three forces which overpower the sinward pull of the carnal mind: (1) A resident grace implanted at the new birth. "Whosoever is born of God doth not commit sin; for his seed remaineth in him: and he cannot sin, because he is born of God."(I John 3:9). (2) Special grace supplied for the crisis of temptation, for we read that "…as thy days, so shall thy strength be." (Deut. 33:25). (3) Man's own dominant assertion that righteousness shall govern his life."

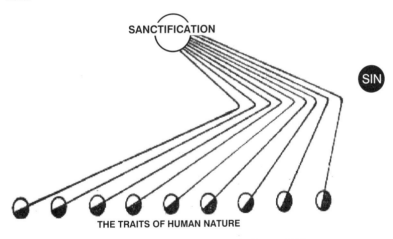

Chart 2. The Disputed Dominion of Grace
"I find then a law, that, when I would do good, evil is present with me."—Romans 7:21*

*We accept the usual interpretation of Romans 7 as setting forth the condition of man under law without grace, but the use of this passage in the present connection is justified by its statement of the conflict between two minds, the mind to sin and the mind to righteousness. In the unregenerate, evil is dominant in the conflict; in the illustration, grace is dominant but its dominance is disputed by sin.

3. The final diagram represents *human nature under the dominion of righteousness*. This man is identified by Paul in I Corinthians 2:15 as the *spiritual* man. This man has experienced a spiritual deliverance and now lives a life of spiritual discernment that enables him to make spiritual discrimination. He has not only been regenerated but also sanctified wholly and has been filled with the Spirit.

Marston said, "Righteousness has here become the law of man's nature, including his every trait, appearing here in white, for the 'mind of the perfect' fully wills the perfect will of God. That the Christian does not perfectly achieve that will is because of human limitations and not because of carnal propensities, for God now functions freely through with no rival within of sin or selfishness."[1]

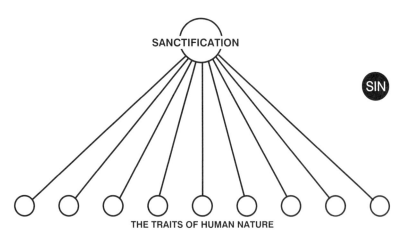

Chart 3. The Dominion of Righteousness
"Sin shall not have dominion over you... But now being made
free from sin, and become servants to God, ye shall have your
fruit unto holiness, and the end everlasting life"
—Romans 6:14 and 22.

1. **Bishop Leslie R. Marston**, *The Wesleyan Message*, printed 1939, Light and Life Press, Marston's Sermon entitled, "The Message for Today."

XVI.

THE IMPORTANCE OF PREACHING HOLINESS

"Holiness is the greatest theme in the Scriptures. Holiness is the foundation and nature of God, and of saints and angels. It is the attribute that rules and controls all of His other attributes. Without holiness God would be unmerciful in His justice and unjust in His mercy; partial in His love, and dangerous in His power. There are only two great moral principles in the universe: sin and holiness. Sin, or anti-holiness is the cause of all our troubles, and holiness is the only cure....If we are to be holiness preachers, it is of *first importance* that we know how to preach holiness."[1]

There are many reasons why we should preach holiness. By "holiness" I mean the doctrine and the experience of entire sanctification and all of its related themes. In a letter to Mr. Merryweather, Wesley wrote, "Where Christian perfection is not strongly and explicitly preached, there is seldom any remarkable blessing from God; and, consequently, little addition to the Society, and little life in the members of it....Till you press the believers to expect full salvation *now*, you must not look for any revival."[2]

God holds the ministry responsible for the condition of the church. To the seven churches of Asia, John, the Revelator, wrote "unto the *angel* (ministers) of the churches." They were and still are responsible for the flock entrusted to their care. There were some in the Old Testament that failed in their responsibility. The Prophet Jeremiah wrote,

"They have healed also the hurt of the daughter of my people slightly, saying, Peace, peace; when there is no peace. Were they ashamed when they had committed abomination? nay, they were not at all ashamed, neither could they blush: therefore they shall fall among them that fall: at the time that I visit them they shall be cast down, saith the Lord." What a judgment awaits them.

On a personal note, I'd like to share the reasons why I want to be faithful to make this truth central in my preaching. When I received my ordination, I vowed to be faithful to the doctrine of holiness as a second work of grace. I made that vow for several reasons: <u>1.</u> Because it was the doctrine that I believed, and the experience that I had received, as well as the life I enjoyed. <u>2.</u> It was the distinguishing doctrine of the Church of the Nazarene, the church through which I found the Lord as my Savior and Sanctifier, and have been a faithful member for nearly 50 years. My faithfulness to the doctrine of 'entire sanctification' is now, not only because of my vow to God but also to His church. If I could not, in all good conscience, be true in preaching holiness, I would be a very dishonest man trying to remain as a minister in good standing in the Church of the Nazarene. My conscience would not permit that kind of disloyalty. <u>3.</u> Because I am a debtor to give the Gospel in the same measure that I received it. <u>4.</u> Because of the supreme price that God paid on Calvary's cross to provide this full salvation. <u>5.</u> Finally, because of His personal call and commission on my life. These are some of the reasons that I am a happy exponent of this great doctrine.

My prayer is that all 'holiness' preachers will make the doctrine of entire sanctification, central in their preaching and not peripheral. It has been recognized that when the ministry of a church is silent on any particular doctrine for a generation, that doctrine, in a very large measure, will be lost to the church. So to preserve the doctrine of entire sanctification and the life of holiness, ministers and teachers must be faithful to proclaim and teach it.

Wesley writing to Mrs. Crosby in 1766 says, "I am afraid Christian perfection should be forgotten....A general faintness, in this respect, is fallen upon this whole kingdom. Sometimes I feel almost weary of striving against the stream both of Preachers and people."[3] Six years later Wesley, to his brother Charles, writes, "I find almost all our Preachers, in every Circuit, have done with Christian perfection. They say, they believe it: But they never preach it; or not once in a quarter. What is to be done? Shall we drop it, or make a point of it."[4] These and many other letters show that Wesley was concerned about the negligence of preaching this truth; we also should be concerned.

Sometime we assume that because people come to our holiness churches they understand its teaching on the subject. But the fact is that people do not have such an understanding of the doctrine. There are also new people attending our services that have never heard it preached and babies being born into our families that need the same teaching that we were privileged to sit under. I'm so thankful that when I came into the church that the preacher did not assume I understood the doctrine of holiness but was faithful in its proclamation so that I could enter into this hallowed relationship with my Lord.

When asked how to preach this doctrine, Wesley responded, "Scarce at all to those who are not pressing forward; to those who are, always by way of promise: always drawing, rather than driving."[5]

The Great Commission that Jesus gave to the church just before He ascended back to the Father, (Acts 1:8), included not only the teaching of the first work of grace but also the second work grace and the whole counsel of God. It is no more irrational to suppose that the heathen world might be evangelized without the preaching of the Gospel, then to suppose that the Christian might be sanctified wholly without the ministry of holiness.

How shall we preach holiness?

Let us preach it experientially, evangelistically, scripturally, logically and theologically. Preach it fearlessly, uncompromisingly, tenderly, practically, seriously, definitely, and constantly. Most of all may we be an example of the message that we proclaim. I remember a preacher saying once that Jesus was the visible expression of the invisible Father, and we are now to be the visible expression of the invisible Christ. May we live, preach, and teach in such a way that the world will see the beauty of Jesus exuding from us.

1. **Arthur L. Vess**, *How to Preach and Teach Holiness*, p. 5

2. **Wesley**, *Letter to Mr. Merryweather*, February 8, 1766 Vol. XII, Letter CCXXXII

3. **Ibid**, *Letter to Mrs. Crosby*, May 3, 1766, Vol. XII, Letter CCCLI

4. **Ibid**, *Letter to Bro. Charles*, March 25, 1772, Vol. XII, Letter LXXXIV

5. **Ibid**, *Plain Account of Christian Perfection*, p. 32